On The Theory And Construction Of Lighthouses

Stevenson, Alan, 1807-1865

1

12.

ON THE

THEORY AND CONSTRUCTION

OF

LIGHTHOUSES.

BY

ALAN STEVENSON, LL.B., F R S E.

FROM THE

EIGHTH EDITION OF THE ENCYCLOPÆDIA BRITANNICA.

EDINBURGH
ADAM AND CHARLES BLACK
MDCCCLVII.

LIGHTHOUSES.

LIGHTHOUSE, and sea-light, are terms which, although not strictly synonymous, are indifferently employed to denote the same thing A *Sea-light* may be defined as *a light so modified and directed as to present to the mariner an appearance which shall at once enable him to judge of his position during the night, in the same manner as the sight of a landmark would do during the day.*

Early history
The early history of lighthouses is very uncertain , and many ingenious antiquaries, finding the want of authentic records, have endeavoured to supply the deficiency by conjectures founded on casual and obscure allusions in ancient writers, and have invented many vague and unsatisfactory hypotheses on the subject, drawn from the heathen mythology Some writers have gone so far as to imagine, that the Cyclopes were the keepers of lighthouses , whilst others have actually maintained that Cyclops was intended, by a bold prosopopœia, to represent a lighthouse itself A notion so fanciful deserves little consideration , and in order to show how ill it accords with that mythology of which it is intended to be an exposition, it seems enough to quote the lines from the ninth Odyssey, where Homer, after describing the darkness of the night, informs us that the fleet of Ulysses actually struck the shore of the Cyclopean island before it could be seen

"Ενθ ουτις την νηϭον ιϭιδϱακιϭ οφθαλμοͥϭιν
Ουτ' ουν κύματα μακϱὰ κυλινδόμινα ϭοϭ` χίϱϭον
Ειϭιδομιν πϱιν νηαϭ ϵ̓υϭϭιλμου, ιϭικιλϭαι

Odyss ix 146

There does not appear any better reason for supposing, that under the history of Tithonus, Chiron, or any other personage of antiquity, the idea of a lighthouse was conveyed , for such suppositions, however reconcileable they may appear with some parts of the mythology, involve obvious inconsistencies with others Nor does it seem at all probable that in those early times, when navigation was so little practised, the advantages of beacon-lights were so generally known and acknowledged as to render them the objects of mythological allegory

Colossus of Rhodes
About 300 years before the Christian era, Chares, the disciple of Lysippus, constructed the celebrated brazen statue, called the Colossus of Rhodes, whose height was upwards of 100 feet, and which stood at the entrance to the harbour.   There is considerable probability in the idea, that this figure served the purposes of a lighthouse , but we do not remember any passage in ancient writers,

where this use of the Colossus is expressly mentioned There is much inconsistency in the account of this fabric by early writers, who, in describing the distant objects which could be seen from it, appear to have forgotten the height which they assign to the figure It was partly demolished by an earthquake, about 80 years after its completion , and so late as the year 672 of our era, the brass of which it was composed was sold by the Saracens to a Jewish merchant of Edessa, for a sum, it is said, equal to L 36,000

Pharos of Alexandria
Little is known with certainty regarding the Pharos of Alexandria, which was regarded by the ancients as one of the seven wonders of the world It was built by Ptolemy Philadelphus, about 300 years before Christ , and it is recorded by Strabo, that the architect Sostratus, the son of Dexiphanes, having first secretly cut his own name on the solid walls of the building, covered the words with plaster, and, in obedience to Ptolemy's command, made the following inscription on the plaster—" King Ptolemy to the gods, the saviours, for the benefit of sailors " What truth there may be in this account of the fraud of Sostratus there is now no means of determining , and the story is only now interesting, in so far as it shows the object of the royal founder and the use of the tower The accounts which have reached us of the dimensions of this remarkable edifice are exceedingly various , and many of the statements regarding the distance at which it could be seen are clearly fabulous Josephus approaches nearest to probability, and informs us, that the fire which was kept constantly burning in the top was visible by seamen at a distance equal to about 40 miles If the reports of some writers are to be believed, this tower must have far exceeded in size the great pyramid itself , but the fact that a building of comparatively so late a date should have so completely disappeared, whilst the pyramid remains almost unchanged, is a sufficient reason for rejecting, as erroneous, the dimensions which have been assigned by most writers to the Pharos of Alexandria.   Some have pretended that large mirrors were employed to direct the rays of the beacon-light on its top in the most advantageous direction , but there is nothing like respectable evidence in favour of this supposition. Others, with greater probability, have imagined that this celebrated beacon was known to mariners, simply by the uncertain and rude light afforded by a common fire In speaking of the Pharos,[1] the poet Lucan, on most occasions

---

[1] Septima nox, Zephyro nunquam laxante rudentes,
Ostendit Pharus Ægyptia littora *flammis*
Sed prius orta dies nocturnam *lampada* texit,
Quam tutas intraret aquas

Pharsal ix, 1004.

Light-
houses.

sufficiently fond of the marvellous, takes no notice of the gigantic mirrors which it is said to have contained. It is true that, by using the word "*lampada*," which can only with propriety be applied to a more perfect mode of illumination than an open fire, he appears to indicate that the "*flamma*" of which he speaks were not so produced. The word *lampada* may, however, be used metaphorically; and *flammis* would, in this case, not improperly describe the irregular appearance of a common fire. Those who are desirous of knowing all that occurs in ancient authors on the subject of the Pharos of Alexandria may consult Pliny, l. xxxvi., c. 12.; l. v., c. 13., and l. xiii, c. 11. Strabo, l. xvii., p. 791, *et seq.* Cæsar, *Comment. de Bell. Civil.*, l. iii. Pompon. Mela, l. ii., c. 7. Ammian. Marcellin, l. xxii., c. 16. Joseph. *de Bell. Judaic.*, l. vi. Nicolas Lloyd's *Lexicon Geographicum*, and the *Notitia Orbis Antiqui* of Celarius, l. iv., c. 1., p. 13.

Coruña Tower.

Mr Moore, in his *History of Ireland* (vol. i., p. 16), speaks of the Tower of Coruña, which, he says, is mentioned in the traditionary history of that country as a lighthouse erected for the use of the Irish in their frequent early intercourse with Spain. In confirmation of this opinion, he cites a somewhat obscure passage from Æthicus, the cosmographer. This in all probability is the tower which Humboldt mentions in his Narrative under the name of the *Iron Tower*, which was built as a lighthouse by Caius Sævius Lupus, an architect of the city of Aqua Flavia, the modern Chaves. A lighthouse has lately been established on this headland, for which dioptric apparatus was supplied from the workshop of M. Létourneau of Paris. (See also a curious account of the traditions about this tower in Southey's *Letters from Spain and Portugal*, p. 17.)

There is also a record in Strabo of a magnificent lighthouse of stone at Capio, or Apio, near the Harbour of Menestheus (the modern Mesa Asta, or Puerto de Sta. Maria), built on a rock nearly surrounded by the sea, as a guide for the shallows at the mouth of the Guadalquivir, which he describes in terms almost identical with those used by him in speaking of the Pharos of Alexandria. I am not aware of any other notice of this great work, for such it seems to have been, to have deserved the praises of Strabo.

In Camden's *Britannia*, a passing notice is taken of the ruins called *Cæsar's Altar*, at Dover, and of the *Tour d'Ordre*, at Boulogne, on the opposite coast; both of which are conjectured, on somewhat doubtful grounds, to have been ancient lighthouses. Pennant describes the remains of a Roman Pharos near Holywell, but cites no authorities for his opinion as to its use. There were likewise remains of a similar structure at Flamborough-head. A very meagre and unintelligible account is also given of a lighthouse at St Edmund's Chapel, on the coast of Norfolk, in Gough's additions to Camden, by which it might seem that the lighthouse was erected in 1272.

Modern history.

Such seems to be the sum of our knowledge of the ancient history of lighthouses, which, it must be admitted, is neither accurate nor extensive. Our information regarding modern lighthouses is of course more minute in its details, and more worthy of credit, as the greater part of it is drawn from authentic sources, or is the result of the actual observation of the writer of this article, who has visited the most important lighthouses of Europe. It seems sufficient here to notice briefly the most remarkable establishments of the kind now in existence; reserving, for the latter part of the article, the more appropriate and important topics of the methods of illumination, and the systems of management.

Tour de Corduan.

The first lighthouse of modern days which merits attention is the Tour de Corduan, which, in point of architec-

tural grandeur, is unquestionably the noblest edifice of the kind in the world. It is situate on an extensive reef at

Light-
houses.

Fig. 1.

the mouth of the River Garonne, and serves as a guide to the shipping of Bordeaux and the Languedoc Canal, and, indeed, of all that part of the Bay of Biscay. It was founded in the year 1584, and was not completed till 1610, under Henri IV. It is minutely described in Belidor's *Architecture Hydralique*. The building is 197 feet in height, and is shown in the accompanying woodcut, fig. 1. Round the base is a wall of circumvallation, 134 feet in diameter, in which the light-keepers' apartments are formed, somewhat in the style of casemates. The first light exhibited in the Tour de Corduan was obtained by burning billets of oak-wood, in a chauffer at the top of the tower; and the use of coal instead of wood was the first improvement which the light received. A rude reflector, in the form of an inverted cone, was afterwards added, to prevent the loss of light which escaped upwards. About the year 1780, M. Lenoir was employed to substitute reflectors and lamps; and in 1822 the light received its last improvement, by the introduction of the dioptric instruments of M. Fresnel.

Eddystone

The history of the celebrated lighthouse on the Eddystone rocks is well known to the general reader, from the narrative of Mr Smeaton the engineer. These rocks are 9¼ miles from the Ram-Head, on the coast of Cornwall; and from the small extent of the surface of the chief rock, and its exposed situation, the construction of the lighthouse was a work of very great difficulty. The first erection was of timber, designed by Mr Winstanley, and was commenced

¹ Oxon, 189.........
² Gough's C .... vol. ii. p. 1.............. at the Dover
Pharos was buil .... Aulus Gaudius .... 3" (Pennant's
History of Whit .... 11.

in 1696 The light was exhibited in November 1698. It was soon found, however, that the sea rose upon this tower to a much greater height than had been anticipated, so much so, it is said, as to "*bury under the water*" the lantern, which was 60 feet above the rock, and Mr Winstanley was therefore afterwards under the necessity of enlarging the tower, and carrying it to the height of 120 feet In November 1703, some considerable repairs were required, and Mr Winstanley, accompanied by his workmen, went to the lighthouse to attend to their execution; but the storm of the 26th of that month carried away the whole erection, when the engineer and all his assistants unhappily perished

The want of a light on the Eddystone soon led to a fatal accident, for, not long after the destruction of Mr Winstanley's lighthouse, the Winchilsea man-of-war was wrecked on the Eddystone rocks, and most of her crew were lost Three years, however, elapsed after this melancholy proof of the necessity of a light before the Trinity House of London could obtain a new act to extend their powers, and it was not till the month of July 1706 that the construction of a new lighthouse was begun, under the direction of Mr John Rudyerd of London On the 28th of July 1708 the new light was first shown, and continued to be regularly exhibited till the year 1755, when the whole fabric was destroyed by accidental fire, after standing 47 years But for this circumstance, it is impossible to tell how long the lighthouse might, with occasional repair, have lasted, as Mr Rudyerd seems to have executed his task with much judgment, carefully rejecting all architectural decoration, as unsuitable for such a situation, and directing his attention to the formation of a tower which should offer the least resistance to the waves The height of the tower, which was of a circular form, and constructed of timber, was, including the lantern, 92 feet, and the diameter at the base, which was a little above the level of high water, was 23

The advantages of a light on the Eddystone having been so long known and acknowledged by seamen, no time was permitted to elapse before active measures were taken for its restoration; and Mr Smeaton, to whom application was

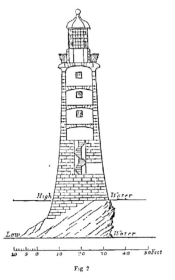

High   *Water*

Low   *Water*

10 5 0   10   20   30   40   50Feet

Fig 2

made for advice on the subject, recommended the exclusive use of stone as the material, which, both from its weight

and other qualities, he considered most suitable for the situation On the 5th of April 1756, Mr Smeaton first landed on the rock, and made arrangements for erecting a lighthouse of stone, and preparing the foundations, by cutting the surface of the rock into regular horizontal benches, into which the stones were carefully dovetailed or notched. The first stone was laid on 12th June 1757, and the last on the 24th of August 1759 The tower measures 68 feet in height, and 26 feet in diameter at the level of the first entire course, and the diameter under the cornice is 15 feet The first 12 feet of the tower form a solid mass of masonry, and the stones are united by means of stone joggles, dovetailed joints, and oak treenails It is remarkable that Mr Smeaton should have adopted an arched form for the floors of his building, instead of employing these floors as tie-walls formed of dovetailed stones To counteract the injurious tendency of the outward thrust of these arched floors, Mr Smeaton had recourse to the ingenious expedient of laying, in circular trenches or beds in the stones which form the outside casing, sets of chains, which were heated by means of an application of hot lead, and became tight in cooling The light was exhibited on the 16th October 1759 but such was the state of the lightroom apparatus in Britain at this period, that a feeble light from tallow candles was all that decorated this noble structure In 1807, when the property of this lighthouse again came into the hands of the Trinity House, on the expiry of a long lease, Argand burners, and parabolic reflectors of silvered copper, were substituted for the chandelier of candles Fig 2 shows a section of the Eddystone lighthouse, as executed according to Mr Smeaton's design

The dangerous reef called the Inch Cape, or Bell-Rock, Bell-Rock. so long a terror to mariners, was well known to the earliest navigators of Scotland Its dangers were so generally acknowledged, that the Abbots of Aberbrothick, from which the rock is distant about 12 miles, caused a float to be fixed upon the rock, with a bell attached to it, which, being swung by the motion of the waves, served by its tolling to warn the mariner of his approach to the reef Amongst the many losses which occurred on the Bell-Rock in modern times, one of the most remarkable is that of the York, 74, with all her crew, part of the wreck having been afterwards found on the rock, and part having come ashore on the neighbouring coast During the survey of the rock also, many instances were discovered of the extent of loss which this reef had occasioned, and many articles of ships' furnishings were picked up on it, as well as various coins, a bayonet, a silver shoe-buckle, and many other small objects Impressed with the great importance of some guide for the Bell-Rock, Captain Brodie, R N, set a small subscription on foot, and erected a beacon of spars on the rock, which, however, was soon destroyed by the sea He afterwards constructed a second beacon, which soon shared the same fate. It was not, however, until 1802, when the Commissioners of Northern Lights brought a bill into parliament for power to erect a lighthouse on it, that any efficient measures were contemplated for the protection of seamen from this rock, which, being covered at every spring-tide to the depth of 12 feet, and lying right in the fareway to the Firths of Forth and Tay, had been the occasion of much loss both of property and life. In 1806 the bill passed into a law, and various ingenious plans were suggested for overcoming the difficulties which were apprehended, in erecting a lighthouse on a rock 12 miles from land, and covered to the depth of 12 feet by the tide But the suggestion of Mr Robert Stevenson, the engineer to the Lighthouse Board, after being submitted to the late Mr Rennie, was at length adopted, and it was determined to construct a tower of masonry, on the principle of the Eddystone On the 17th of August 1807, Mr Stevenson accordingly landed with his workmen, and commenced the work by preparing

the rock to receive the supports of a temporary wooden pyramid, on which a barrack-house, for the reception of the
workmen, was to be placed, and during this operation much
hazard was often incurred in transporting the men from the
rock, which was only dry for a few hours at spring-tides,
to the vessel which lay moored off it   The lowest floor of
this temporary erection, in which the mortar for the building
was prepared, was often broken up and removed by the force
of the sea   The foundation having been excavated, the
first stone was laid on the 10th July 1808, at the depth of
16 feet below the high-water of spring-tides, and at the
end of the second season, the building was 5 feet 6 inches
above the lowest part of the foundation   The third season's
operations terminated by finishing the solid part of the
structure, which is 30 feet in height, and the whole of
the masonry was completed in October 1810   The light
was first exhibited to the public on the night of the 1st of
February 1811.   The difficulties and hazards of this work
were chiefly caused by the short time during which the
rock was accessible between the ebbing and flowing tides,
and amongst the many eventful incidents which rendered
the history of this work interesting was the narrow escape
which the engineer and thirty-one persons made from being
drowned, by the rising of the tide upon the rock, before a
boat came to their assistance, the attending vessel having
broken adrift   This circumstance occurred before the barrack-house was erected, and is narrated by Mr Stevenson
in his account of the work, published at the expense of the
Lighthouse Board in 1824, to which we may refer for more
minute information on the subject of this work, and the
other lights of the coast of Scotland

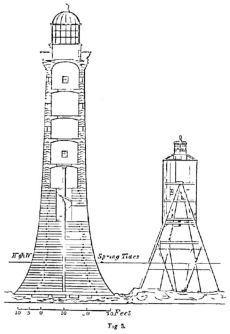

H'gh W'.   Spring Tides.

10 5 0   10   20   70 Feet

Fig 3.

The Bell-Rock Tower is 100 feet in height, 42 feet in

diameter at the base, and 15 at the top   The door is 30
feet from the base, and the ascent is by a massive copper
ladder   The apartments including the light-room, are six
in number   The light is a revolving red and white light,
and is produced by the revolution of a frame containing 20
Argand lamps, placed in the foci of parabolic mirrors, arranged on a quadrangular frame, whose alternate faces have
shades of red glass placed before the reflectors, so that a
red and white light is shown successively   The machinery,
which causes the revolution of the frame containing the
lamps, is also applied to tolling two large bells, to give
warning to the mariner of his approach to the rock in foggy
weather.   Fig 3 shows a section of the Bell-Rock Lighthouse, and of the temporary barrack-house, which was removed on the completion of the work   The entire cost of
the lighthouse was L 61,331, 9s 2d

The great merit of Mr Stevenson, as architect of the
Bell-Rock Lighthouse, lies in his bold conception and un-
shaken belief in the possibility of erecting a tower of masonry on a reef 12 miles from the nearest land, and covered
by every tide,—a situation, undoubtedly, much more difficult than that of the Eddystone   But his mechanical skill
in carrying on the work is also deserving of high praise
Not only did he conceive the plan of the *moveable jib* and
balance cranes which he afterwards used with much advantage in building the tower, but his zeal, ever alive to the
possibility of improving on the conceptions of his great
master Smeaton, led him to introduce several beneficial
changes into the arrangements of the masonry   In particular, he converted the stone floors of the apartments,
which in the Eddystone exert an *outward*, and in its tendency disruptive, thrust, into bonds of union and efficient
sources of stability   This thrust was by Smeaton himself
considered so disadvantageous, that he thought fit to counteract it, as already noticed, by means of metallic *girders*,
concealed in the stone-work, and most ingeniously applied
The Lighthouse Board placed in the upper apartment of
the tower a bust of Mr Stevenson, " in testimony," as the
minutes record, " of the sense entertained by the Commissioners of his distinguished talent and indefatigable zeal in
the erection of the Lighthouse '

The most remarkable lighthouse on the coast of Ireland
is that of Carlingford, near Cranfield Point at the entrance
of Carlingford Lough   It was built according to the design
of Mr George Halpin the Inspector of the Irish Lights,
and was a work of an arduous nature, being founded twelve
feet below the level of high-water on the Hawlbowline
Rock, which lies about two miles off Cranfield Point   The
figure is that of a frustum of a cone, 111 feet in height, and
48 feet in diameter at the base   The light, which is fixed,
is from oil burned in Argand lamps placed in the foci of
parabolic mirrors   It was first exhibited on the night of the
20th December 1830

The Skerryvore Rocks, which lie about 12 miles W S W.
of the seaward point of the Isle of Tyree, in Argyllshire,
were long known as a terror to mariners, owing to the
numerous shipwrecks, fatal alike to the vessels and the
crews, which had occurred in their neighbourhood   A list
confessedly incomplete, enumerates thirty vessels lost in the
forty years preceding 1844, but how many others, which
during that period had been reported as " foundered at sea "
or as to whose fate not even an opinion has been hazarded,
may have been wrecked on this dangerous reef, which lies
so much in the track of the shipping of Liverpool and the
Clyde, it would be vain to conjecture [1]   The Commissioners
of the Northern Lighthouses had for many years entertained the project of erecting a lighthouse on the Skerry-

Carling-
ford

Skerryvore
Rocks

vore; and with this object had visited it, more especially in the year 1814, in company with Sir Walter Scott, who, in

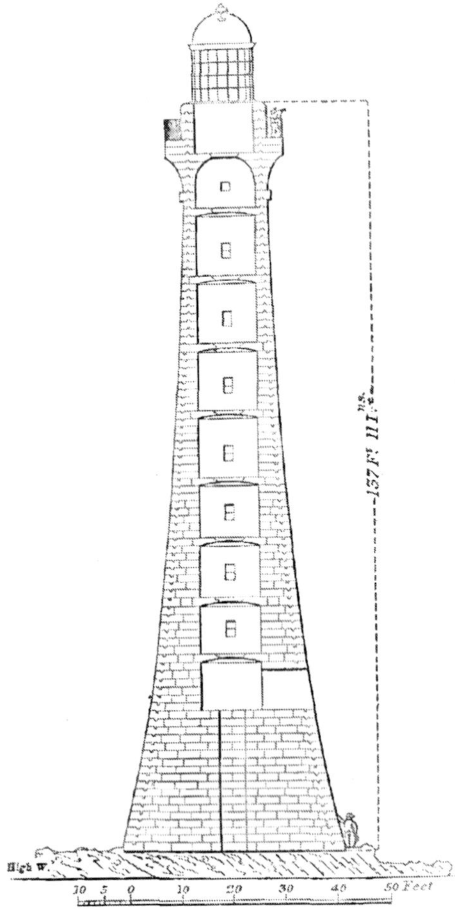

Fig. 4.

his diary, gives a graphic description of its inhospitable aspect. The great difficulty of landing on the rock, which is worn smooth by the continual beat of Atlantic waves, which rise with undiminished power from the deep water near it, held out no cheering prospect; and it was not until the year 1834, when a minute survey of the reef was ordered by the Board, that the idea of commencing this formidable work was seriously embraced.

The reef is composed of numerous rocks, stretching over a surface of nearly 8 miles from W.S.W. to E.N.E. The main *nucleus*, which alone presents sufficient surface for the base of a lighthouse, is nearly 3 miles from the seaward end of the cluster. It is composed of a very compact *gneiss*, worn smooth as glass by the incessant play of the waters, and is so small that at high-water little remains around the base of the tower but a narrow band of a few feet in width, and some rugged humps of rock, separated by gullies,

through which the sea plays almost incessantly. The cutting of the foundation for the tower in this irregular flinty mass occupied nearly two summers; and the blasting of the rock, in so narrow a space, without any shelter from the risk of flying splinters, was attended with much hazard.

In such a situation as that of Skerryvore everything was to be provided beforehand and transported from a distance; and the omission in the list of wants of even a little clay for the *tamping* of the mine-holes might for a time have entirely stopped the works. Barracks were to be built at the workyard in the neighbouring Island of Tyree, and also in the Isle of Mull, where the granite for the tower was quarried. Piers were also built in Mull and Tyree for the shipment and landing of materials; and at the latter place a harbour or basin, with a reservoir and sluices for scouring the entrance, were formed for the accommodation of the small vessel which attends the lighthouse. It was, besides, found necessary, in order to expedite the transport of the building materials from Tyree and Mull to Skerryvore Rock, to build a steam-tug, which also served, in the early stages of the work, as a floating barrack for the workmen. In that branch of the service she ran many risks, while she lay moored off the rock in a perilous anchorage, with *two-thirds* of the horizon of *foul ground*, and a rocky and deceitful bottom, on which the anchor often *tripped*.

The operations at Skerryvore were commenced in the summer of 1838, by placing on the rock a wooden barrack, similar to that first used by Mr Robert Stevenson at the Bell-Rock. (See Fig. 3.) The framework was erected in the course of the season on a part of the rock as far removed as possible from the proposed foundation of the lighthouse tower; but in the great gale which occurred on the night of the 3d of November following, it was entirely destroyed and swept from the rock, nothing remaining to point out its site but a few broken and twisted iron stancheons, and attached to one of them a piece of a beam, so *shaken* and rent by dashing against the rock as literally to resemble a bunch of laths. Thus did one night obliterate the traces of a season's toil, and blast the hopes which the workmen fondly cherished of a stable dwelling on the rock, and of refuge from the miseries of sea-sickness, which the experience of the season had taught many of them to dread more than death itself. After the removal of the roughest part of the foundation of the tower had been nearly completed, during almost two entire seasons, by the party of men who lived on board the vessel while she lay moored off the rock, a second and successful attempt was made to place another barrack of the same description, but strengthened by a few additional iron ties, and a centre post, in a part of the rock less exposed to the breach of the heaviest waves than the site of the first barrack had been. This second house braved the storm for several years after the works were finished, when it was taken down and removed from the rock, to prevent any injury from its sudden destruction by the waves. " Perched 40 feet above the wave-beaten rock, in this singular abode," says Mr Alan Stevenson, the engineer, "with a goodly company of thirty men, I have spent many a weary day and night at those times when the sea prevented any one going down to the rock, anxiously looking for supplies from the shore, and earnestly longing for a change of weather favourable to the recommencement of the works. For miles around nothing could be seen but white foaming breakers, and nothing heard but howling winds and lashing waves. At such seasons much of our time was spent in bed; for there alone we had effectual shelter from the winds and the spray, which searched every cranny in the walls of the barrack. Our slumbers, too, were at times fearfully interrupted by the sudden pouring of the sea over the roof, the rocking of the house on its pillars, and the spurting of water through the seams of the doors and windows—symptoms which, to one suddenly aroused from sound sleep recalled the appalling fate of the former barrack, which had been engulphed in the foam not twenty yards from our dwelling, and for a moment seemed to summon us to a similar fate On two occasions, in particular," says the engineer, " those sensations were so vivid as to cause almost every one to spring out of bed , and some of the men fled from the barrack, by a temporary gangway, to the more stable but less comfortable shelter afforded by the bare wall of the light-house tower, then unfinished, where they spent the remainder of the night in the darkness and the cold."

The design for the Skerryvore Lighthouse was given by Mr Alan Stevenson, and is an adaptation of Smeaton's Eddy-stone Tower to the peculiar situation and the circumstances of the case at the Skerryvore with such modifications in the general arrangements and dimensions of the building as the enlarged views of the importance of lighthouses which pre-vail in the present day seemed to call for

The tower is 138 feet 6 inches high, and 42 feet in dia-meter at the base, and 16 feet at the top It contains a mass of stone-work of about 58,580 cubic feet, or more than *double* that of the Bell-Rock, and not much less than *five times* that of the Eddystone The lower part of the tower was built by means of *jib-cranes*, and the upper part with *shear-poles, needles*, and a balance-crane The shear-poles were similar to those used by Smeaton at the Eddystone , and the *jib-cranes* and *balance-crane* were the same as those which were designed and first employed by Mr Robert Stevenson in the erection of the Bell-Rock Lighthouse The mortar used was compounded of equal parts of lime-stone (from the Halkin Mountain, near Holywell, in North Wales), burnt and ground at the works, and of Pozzolano earth The light of Skerryvore is revolving, and reaches its brightest state *once every minute* It is produced by the revolution of eight great annular lenses around a central lamp with four wicks, and belongs to the first order of diop-tric lights in the system of Fresnel The light may be seen from a vessel's deck at the distance of 18 miles The en-tire cost of the lighthouse, including the purchase of the steam-vessel, and the building of the harbour at Hynish for the reception of the small vessel, which now attends the lighthouse, was L 86,977, 17s 7d

" In such a situation as the Skerryvore," says the en-gineer, " innumerable delays and disappointments were to be expected by those engaged in the work ; and the entire loss of the fruit of the first season's labour in the course of a few hours was a good lesson in the school of patience, and of trust in something better than an arm of flesh During our progress, also, cranes and other materials were swept away by the waves, vessels were driven by sudden gales to seek shelter at a distance from the rocky shores of Mull and Tyree, and the workmen were left on the rock desponding and idle, and destitute of many of the comforts with which a more roomy and sheltered dwelling, and the neighbourhood of friends, are generally connected Daily risks were run in landing on the rock in a heavy surf, in blasting the splintery gneiss, or by the falling of heavy bodies from the tower on the narrow space below, to which so many persons were ne-cessarily confined Yet had we not any loss of either life or limb , and although our labours were prolonged from dawn to night, and our provisions were chiefly salt, the health of the people, with the exception of a few slight cases of dysentery, was generally good throughout the six suc-cessive summers of our sojourn on the rock The close of the work was welcomed with thankfulness by all engaged in it , and our remarkable preservation was viewed, even by many of the most thoughtless as, in a peculiar manner, the gracious work of Him by whom ' the very hairs of our heads are all numbered ' "

There can be little doubt that, down to a very late pe-riod, the only mode of illumination adopted in the light-houses, even of the most civilized nations of Europe, was the combustion of wood or coal in a chauffer on the top of a high tower It is needless to enlarge upon the evils of such a method , they need only be named to be understood, for it is difficult to conceive how an efficient system of lighting a coast could be managed under such disadvan-tages The uncertainty caused by the effects of wind and rain, and the impossibility of rendering one light distin-guishable from another, must have at all times rendered the early lighthouses in a great measure useless to the mariner

M Teulère, a member of the Royal Corps of Engineers of Bridges and Roads in France, is, by some, considered the first who hinted at the advantages of parabolic reflectors , and he is said, in a memoir dated the 26th June 1783, to have proposed their combination with Argand lamps, ranged on a revolving frame, for the Corduan lighthouse. What-ever foundation there may be for the claim of M Teulère, certain it is, that this plan was actually carried into effect at Corduan under the directions of the Chevalier Borda, and to him is generally awarded the merit of having conceived the idea of applying parabolic mirrors to lighthouses These were prodigious steps in the improvement of lighthouses, as not only the power of the lights was thus greatly increased, but the introduction of a revolving frame proved a valuable source of distinction amongst lights, and has since been the means of greatly extending their utility. The exact date of the change on the light of the Corduan is not known , but as it was made by Lenoir, the same young artist to whom Borda, about the year 1780, intrusted the construction of his reflecting circle, it has been conjectured by some that the improvement was made about the same time If this conjecture be correct, the claim of M Teulère must of course fall to the ground The reflectors were formed of sheet copper, plated with silver, and had a double ordinate of 31 French inches It was not long before these improve-ments were adopted in England by the Trinity House of London, who sent a deputation to France to inquire into their nature In Scotland, one of the first acts of the Northern Lights Board, in 1786, was to substitute reflectors in the room of coal lights, then in use at the Isle of May in the Firth of Forth, and the Cumbrae Isle in the Firth of Clyde, which had, till that period, been the only beacons on the Scotch coast The reflectors employed were formed of facets of mirror glass, placed in hollow parabolical moulds of plaster, according to the designs of the late Mr Thomas Smith, the engineer of the Board, who, as appears from the article *Reflector* in the Supplement to the third edition of the Encyclopædia Britannica, was not aware of what had been done in France, and had, himself, conceived the idea of this combination The system of Borda was also adopted in Ireland, and, in time, variously modified, it became gene-ral wherever lighthouses were known.

The property of the parabola, by which all lines incident on its surface from the focus make with normals to the curve at the points of incidence, angles equal to the inclination of these same normals respectively to lines drawn parallel to the axis of the curve, is that which fits it for the purposes of a lighthouse A hollow mirror, formed by the revolu-tion of a portion of a parabola about its axis, has, in conse-quence of this property, the power of projecting the repeated images of a luminous point placed in its focus, in directions parallel to the axis of the generating curve , so that, when the mirror is placed with its axis parallel to the horizon, a cylindric beam of light is thereby sent forward in a horizon-tal direction When such mirrors are placed side by side, with their axes parallel on the face of a quadrangular frame which revolves about a vertical axis, a distant observer re-ceives the successive impressions which result from the passage of each face of the frame over a line drawn between the observer's eye and the centre of the revolving frame. This arrangement constitutes what is called a revolving light. A fixed light is produced by placing, side by side, round a circular frame, a number of reflectors, with their axes inclined to each other, so as to be radii containing equal arcs of the frame on which they are placed. It is obvious that a perfect parabolic figure, and a luminous *point* mathematically true, would render the illumination of the whole horizon by means of a fixed light *impossible*, and it is only from the aberration caused by the size of the flame which is substituted for the point, that we are enabled to render even revolving lights practically useful. But for this aberration, even the slowest revolution in a revolving light, which would be consistent with a continued observable series, such as the practical seaman could follow, would render the flashes of a revolving light greatly too transient for any useful purpose, whilst fixed lights, being visible in the azimuths only in which the mirrors are placed, would, over the greater part of the distant horizon, be altogether invisible. The size of the flame, therefore, which is placed in the focus of a parabolic mirror, when taken in connection with the form of the mirror itself, leads to those important modifications in the paths of the rays, and the form of the resultant beam of light, which have rendered the catoptric system of lights so great a benefit to the benighted seaman.

It is obvious, from a consideration of the nature of the action which takes place in this combination of the paraboloidal mirrors with Argand lamps, that the revolving light is not only more perfect in its nature than the fixed light, but that it possesses the advantage of being susceptible of an increase of its power, by increasing the number of reflectors, which have their axes parallel to each other, so as to concentrate the effect of several mirrors in one direction. The perfect parallelism of the axes of separate mirrors, it is true, is unattainable, but approaches may be made sufficiently near for practical results, and in order to prolong the duration of the flash, the reflectors are sometimes placed on a frame, having each of its sides slightly convex, by which arrangement the outer reflectors of each face of the frame have their axes less inclined inwards from the radii of the revolving frame which pass through their foci.

The best proportions for the paraboloidal mirrors depend upon the object to which they are to be applied, as mirrors which are intended to produce great divergence in the form of the resultant beam should have one form, whilst those which are designed to cause a near approach to parallelism of the rays will have another form. These objects may also be attained by variations of the size of the flame applied in the same mirror, but it is much more advantageous to produce the effect by a change in the form of the mirror, as any increase of the flame beyond the size which is found to be most advantageous in other respects cannot be regarded otherwise than as a wasteful expenditure of light. The details into which a full investigation of this matter would lead us are quite beyond the scope of this article, and it therefore seems sufficient to give the formula which express the relations which exist between the size of the flame, the reflecting surface, and the corresponding divergence of the reflected ray. If Δ represent the inclination of any reflected ray to the axis of a paraboloidal mirror, e the distance of the focus from the point of reflection, and d the distance from the edge of the flame to the focus in the plane of reflection, we shall have sine $\Delta = \dfrac{d}{e}$, and when the flame in the given plane of reflection is circular, or has its opposite sides equidistant from the focus of the mirror, we shall, by putting Δ' for the effective divergence of the mirror in the given plane, have $\Delta' = 2\Delta$. When, there-

fore, great divergence, as in the case of the fixed lights, is required, the prolate form of the curve is to be preferred, and the oblate is conversely more suited to revolving lights.

The power of the reflectors ordinarily employed in lighthouses is generally equal to about 360 times the effect of the unassisted flame which is placed in the focus. This value, however, is strictly applicable only at the distances at which the observations have been made, as the proportional value of the reflected beam must necessarily vary with the distance of the observer, agreeably to some law dependent upon the unequal distribution of the light in the luminous cone which proceeds from it. The ordinary burners used in lighthouses are one inch in diameter, and the focal distance generally adopted is four inches, so that the effective divergence of the mirror in the horizontal plane may be estimated at about 14° 22'. In arranging reflectors on the frame of a fixed light, however, it would be advisable to calculate upon less effective divergence, for beyond 11° the light is feeble, but the difficulty of placing many mirrors on one frame, and the great expense of oil required for so many lamps, have generally led to the adoption of the first valuation of the divergence.

The reflectors used in the best lighthouses are made of sheet copper plated, in the proportion of 6 oz. of silver to 16 oz. of copper. They are moulded to the paraboloidal form by a delicate and laborious process of beating with mallets and hammers, of various forms and materials, and are frequently tested during the operation by the application of a carefully-formed mould. After being brought to the curve, they are stiffened by means of a strong beazle, and a strap of brass, which is attached to it for the purpose of preventing any accidental alteration of its figure. Polishing powders are then applied, and the instrument receives its last finish.

Two gauges of brass are applied to test the form of the reflector. One is for the back, and is used by the workmen during the process of hammering, and the other is applied to the concave face as a test, while the mirror is receiving its final polish. It is then tested, by tying a burner in the focus, and measuring the intensity of the light at various points of the reflected conical beam. Another test may also be applied successively to various points in the surface, by masking the rest of the mirror. Having placed a screen in the line of the axis of the mirror at some given distance from it, it is easy to find whether the image of a very small object placed in the conjugate focus, which is due to the distance of the screen, be reflected at any distance from that point on the centre of the screen through which the prolongation of the axis of the mirror would pass, and thus to obtain a measure of the error of the instrument. For this purpose it is necessary to find the position of the conjugate focus, which corresponds to the distance of the screen. If b be the distance which the object should be removed outwards from the principal focus of the mirror, d the distance from the focus to the screen, and r the distance from the focus to the point of the mirror which is to be tested, we shall have $b = \dfrac{r^2}{d}$ as the distance which the

object must be removed outwards from the true focus on the line of the axis.

The flame generally used in reflectors is from an Argand fountain-lamp, whose wick is an inch in diameter. Much care is bestowed upon the manufacture of these lamps for the Northern Lighthouses, which have their burners tipped with silver, to prevent wasting by the great heat which is evolved. These burners are also fitted with a slide apparatus, accurately turned, by which the burner may be removed from the interior of the mirror at the time of cleaning it, and returned exactly to the same place, and locked by means of a key. This arrangement, which is shown in figs. 5, 6, and 7, is very important, as it ensures the burner always being in the focus, and does not require the reflector to be lifted out of its place every time it is cleaned; so that, when once carefully set and screwed down to the frame, it is never altered. In these figs. *aaa* represents one of the reflectors, *b* is the lamp, *c* is a cylindric fountain, which contains 24 oz. of oil. The oil-pipe and fountain of the former is connected with the rectangular frame *d*, and is moveable in a vertical direction upon the guide-rods *e* and *f*, by

Fig. 5.

which it can be let down and taken out of the reflector by simply turning the handle *g*, as will be more fully understood by examining fig. 6. An aperture of an elliptical form, measuring about 2 inches by three, is cut in the upper and lower part of the reflector, the lower serving for the free egress and ingress of the lamp, and the upper, to which the copper tube *h* is attached, serving for ventilation; *i* shows a cross section of the main bar of the chandelier or frame, on which the reflectors are ranged, each being made to rest on knobs of brass, one of which is seen at *kk*, and which are soldered on the brass band *l*, that clasps the exterior of the reflector. Fig. 5 is a section of the reflector *aa*, showing the position of the burner *b*, with the glass chimney *b'*, and oil-cup *l*, which receives any oil that may drop from the lamp. Fig. 6 shows the apparatus for moving

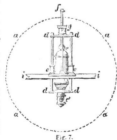

Fig. 6.

the lamp up and down, so as to remove it from the reflector at the time of cleaning it. In the diagram, *c*, the fountain, is moved partly down; *dd* shows the rectangular frame on which the burner is mounted, *e, e* the elongated socket-guides, *f* the rectangular guide-rod, connected with the perforated sockets on which the *checking-handle g* slides.

The modes of arranging the reflectors in the frames are shown in figs. 8, 9, and 10. It seems quite unnecessary, after what is said on the subject of divergence,

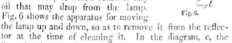

Fig. 7.

to do more than remark, that in revolving lights the reflectors are placed with their axes parallel to each other, so as to concentrate their power in one direction; whilst in fixed lights it is necessary, in order to effect as equal a distribution of the light over the horizon as possible, to place the reflectors, with their axes inclined to each other at an angle somewhat less than that of the divergence of the reflected cone. For this purpose a brass gauge, composed of two long arms, somewhat in the form of a pair of common dividers, connected by means of a graduated limb, is employed. The arms having been first placed at the angle, which is supplemental to that required (i.e. the half of the two adjacent inclinations are to be set off in the centre of the reflector), one of the arms is moved up, and whilst its edges are in close contact with that arm as the faces of the arms

of the gauge. The different arrangements of the reflectors will be more fully understood by referring to the figures.

Figs. 8 and 10 show an elevation and plan of a revolving apparatus on the catoptric principle. In these figures, *nn*, shows the reflector frame or chandelier; *o, o*, the reflectors with their oil-fountains *p, p*. The whole is attached to the revolving axis or shaft *q*. The copper tubes, *r, r*, convey the smoke from the lamps; *s, s* are cross bars which support the shaft at *tt*; *uu* is a copper pan for receiving any moisture which may accidentally enter at the central ventilator in the roof of the light-room; *l* is a cast-iron bracket, which supports the pivot on the shaft; *m, m* are bevelled wheels, which convey motion from the machine to the shaft. Fig. 9 shows a plan of one tier of

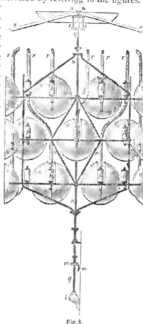

Fig. 8.

reflectors arranged in the manner employed in a fixed catoptric light; *nn* shows the chandelier, *q* the fixed shaft in the

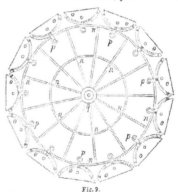

Fig. 9.

centre, which supports the whole, *o, o* the reflectors, and *p, p* the fountains of their lamps.

A variety of the parabolic reflectors has been invented by M. Bordier Marcet, the pupil and successor of Argand, who has laboured with much enthusiasm in perfecting catoptric instruments, more especially with a view to their application to the illumination of lighthouses and the streets of towns. Amongst many other ingenious combinations of parabolic mirrors, he has invented and constructed an apparatus, which is much used in harbour-lights on the French coast. The object of these mirrors is to fulfil, as nearly as possible, the conditions required in a fixed light, by illuminating with equal intensity every part of the horizon, by means of a fixed mirror; and M. Bordier

Light-
houses

Marcet has in his workshop an instrument of this kind, 8 feet in diameter, which he constructed on speculation The apparatus used in harbour-lights, on the French coast, is of much smaller dimensions, and does not exceed 15 inches in diameter A perfect idea of the construction and effect of this apparatus may be formed by conceiving a parabola to revolve about its parameter as an axis, so that its upper and lower limbs would become the generat-

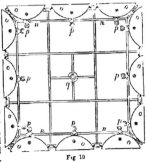

Fig 10

ing lines of two surfaces possessing the property of reflecting, in lines parallel to the axis of the parabola, all the rays incident upon them, from a light placed in the point where the parameter and axis of the generating parabola intersect each other This point being the focus of each parabolic section of this apparatus, the light is equally dispersed in every point of the horizon, when the axes of the parabolic sections are in a plane perpendicular to a vertical line But, however perfectly this apparatus may attain this important object, it does so at the sacrifice of the most efficient part of the parabolic surface, which lies between the vertex and the parameter, and therefore produces a proportionally feeble effect. This beautiful little instrument is shown in fig 11, in which b shows the burner, pp

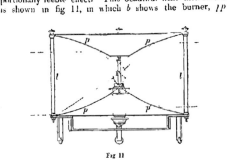

Fig 11

the upper reflecting surface, and $p'p'$ the lower reflecting surface, both generated in the manner above described, by the revolution of a parabola, about its parameter ab, F is the focus of the generating parabola, and l, l are small pillars which connect the two reflecting plates, and give strength to the apparatus

Spherical mirrors

Spherical mirrors are employed in lighthouses only as subsidiary parts in dioptric apparatus, and any observations regarding them will, therefore, be made in treating of the dioptric lights of Fresnel.

Floating lights

Floating lights are only resorted to in cases of absolute necessity, as their maintenance is extremely expensive, whilst they are less to be relied on, and, in all respects, less efficient than land lights They are large vessels, built with great breadth of beam, and are generally moored off shoals, or serve as guides for taking channels The lights are from lamps placed in front of small reflectors, ranged in lanterns which are hoisted on the masts of the vessel

Light-
houses

Distinc-
tions of
catoptric
lights

Catoptric lights are susceptible of nine separate distinctions, which are called *fixed*, *revolving white*, *revolving red and white*, *revolving red with two whites*, *revolving white with two reds*, *flashing*, *intermittent*, *double fixed lights*, *and double revolving lights* The first exhibits a steady and uniform appearance, which is not subject to any change, and the reflectors used for it are of smaller dimensions than those employed in revolving lights This is necessary, in order to permit them to be ranged round the circular frame, with their axes inclined at such an angle as shall enable them to illuminate every point of the horizon The revolving light is produced by the revolution of a frame with three or four sides, having reflectors of a large size grouped on each side, with their axes parallel, and as the revolution exhibits a light gradually increasing to *full strength*, and in the same gradual manner decreasing to total darkness, its appearance is extremely well marked The succession of *red* and *white* lights is caused by the revolution of a frame whose different sides present red and white lights, and these, as already mentioned, afford three separate distinctions, namely, alternate red and white, the succession of two white lights after one red, and the succession of two red lights after one white light The *flashing* light is produced in the same manner as the *revolving* light, but owing to a different construction of the frame, and the greater quickness of the revolution, a totally different and very striking effect is produced The brightest and darkest periods being but momentary, this light is characterized by a rapid succession of bright flashes, from which it gets its name The *intermittent* light is distinguished by bursting suddenly into view, and continuing steady for a short time, after which it is suddenly eclipsed for half a minute Its striking appearance is produced by the perpendicular motion of circular shades in front of the reflectors, by which the light is alternately hid and displayed This distinction, as well as that called the *flashing light*, are peculiar to the Scotch coast, having been first introduced by Mr R Stevenson, the late engineer of the Northern Lights Board The double lights, which are generally used only where there is a necessity for a *leading* line, as a guide for taking some channel, or avoiding some danger, are exhibited from two towers, one of which is higher than the other, and when seen in one line, form a direction for the course of shipping At the Calf of Man a striking variety has been introduced into the character of leading lights, by substituting for two *fixed* lights, two lights which revolve in the same periods, and exhibit their flashes at the same instant, and these lights are, of course, susceptible of every variety enumerated above, that of two revolving red and white lights revolving in equal periods The utility of all these distinctions is chiefly to be imputed to their at once striking the eye of an observer, and being instantaneously obvious to strangers

¹ Dioptric system of Fresnel

Before entering upon the subject of the dioptric lights, the writer of this article embraces with pleasure the opportunity afforded to him of acknowledging the liberality of M Léonor Fresnel, the late Secretary of the Lighthouse Commission of France It was entirely owing to the readiness with which M Fresnel afforded him access to every avenue of information on the subject of lighthouses that he was enabled to effect the object of a mission to France, on which he was sent in the year 1834, by the Commissioners of Northern Lights

The first proposal of applying lenses to lighthouses is recorded by Smeaton in his account of the Eddystone Lighthouse, where he mentions that, in 1759, an optician in London proposed grinding the glass of the lantern to a radius of seven feet six inches, but the description is too vague to admit of even a conjecture regarding the proposed arrangement of the apparatus. About forty years ago, however, lenses were actually tried in several lighthouses in the south of England, but their imperfect figure, and the quantity of light absorbed by the glass, which was of inferior quality and of considerable thickness, rendered their effect so much inferior to that of the parabolic reflectors then in use, that, after trying some strange combinations of lenses and reflectors, the former were finally abandoned.

The object to be attained by the use of lenses in a lighthouse is, of course, identical with that which is answered by employing reflectors; and both instruments effect the same end by different means, collecting the rays which diverge from a point called the *focus*, and projecting them forward in a beam, whose axis coincides with the produced axis of the instrument. The actions by which these similar results are effected have been termed *reflection* and *refraction*. In the one case the light, as has been already said, merely impinges on the reflecting surface, and is thrown back; whilst in the other, the rays pass through the refracting medium, and are bent or refracted from their natural course.

The celebrated Buffon, to prevent the great absorption of light by the thickness of the material, which would necessarily result from giving to a lens of great dimensions a figure continuously spherical, proposed to grind out of a solid piece of glass a lens in steps or concentric zones. This suggestion of Buffon, regarding the construction of large burning glasses, was first executed, with tolerable success, about the year 1780, by the Abbé Rochon; but such are the difficulties attending the process of working a solid piece of glass into the necessary form, that it is believed the only other instrument ever constructed in this manner is that which was made by Messrs Cookson of Newcastle-upon-Tyne, for the Commissioners of Northern Lighthouses.

The merit of having first suggested the building of these lenses in separate pieces seems to be due to Condorcet, who in his *Éloge de Buffon*, published so far back as 1773, enumerates the advantages to be derived from this method.[1] Sir David Brewster also described this mode of building lenses in 1811, in the *Edinburgh Encyclopædia*, and in 1822, the late eminent Fresnel, alike unacquainted with the suggestions of Condorcet, or the description by Sir David Brewster, explained, with many ingenious and interesting details, the same mode of constructing these instruments. To Fresnel belongs the additional merit of having first followed up his invention by the construction of a lens, and, in conjunction with MM. Arago and Mathieu, of placing a powerful lamp in its focus, and, indeed, of finally applying it to the practical purposes of a lighthouse. The fertile genius of the French Academician has produced many ingenious combinations of dioptric instruments for lighthouses, which we shall have occasion to notice in the sequel.

The great advantages which attend the mode of construction proposed by Condorcet are, the ease of execution, by which a more perfect figure may be given to each zone, and spherical aberration almost entirely corrected, and the power of forming a lens of larger dimensions than could easily be made from a solid piece. Buffon appears only to have had in view the reduction of the thickness of the lens, but Condorcet distinctly suggests the possibility of correcting the spherical aberration by properly selected centres for the various zones.

To Fresnel, however, is due the credit of having determined these centres, which constantly recede from the axis of the lens in proportion as the zones to which they refer are removed from its centre, and the surfaces of the zones of the annular lens, consequently, are not parts of concentric spheres, as in Buffon's lens. It deserves notice, that the first lenses constructed for Fresnel by M. Soleil had their zones polygonal, so that the surfaces were not annular, a form which Fresnel considered less accommodated to the ordinary resources of the optician. He also, with his habitual penetration, preferred the plano-convex to the double-convex form, as more easily executed. After mature consideration, he finally adopted crown glass, which, notwithstanding its greenish colour, he considered more suitable than flint glass, as being less liable to *striæ*. All his calculations were made in reference to an index of refraction of 1.51, which he had verified by repeated experiments, conducted with that patience and accuracy for which, amidst his higher qualities, he was so remarkably distinguished. These instruments have received the name of *annular* lenses, from the figure of the surface of the zones.

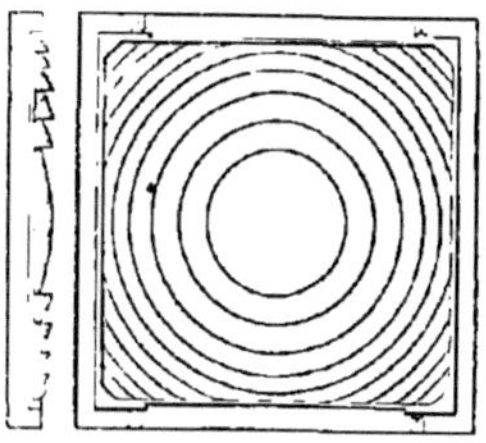

Fig 12

Fig. 12 exhibits a plan and section of an annular lens of the largest size, whose focal distance is 92 centimetres, or about 36.22 inches, and which subtends a luminous pyramid of 46° of inclination, having its apex in the flame.

Having once contemplated the possibility of illuminating lighthouses by dioptric means, Fresnel quickly perceived the advantage of employing for fixed lights a lamp placed in the centre of a polygonal hoop, consisting of a series of cylindric refractors, *infinitely small* in their length, and having their axes in planes parallel to the horizon.

Such a continuation of vertical cylindric sections of various curvatures, by refracting the rays proceeding from the focus only in a direction perpendicular to the vertical sections of the cylindric parts, must distribute a zone of light *equally brilliant* in every point of the horizon. This effect will be easily understood, by considering the middle vertical section of one of the great annular lenses or burning glasses, already described, abstractly from its relation to the rest of the instrument. It will readily be perceived that this section possesses the property of refracting the rays in the vertical plane only, without interfering with azimuthal divergence; and if this section, by its revolution about a vertical axis becomes the generating line of the enveloping hoop above noticed, such a hoop would of course possess the property of refracting an equally diffused zone of light round the horizon. The difficulty, however, of forming this apparatus, appeared so great, that Fresnel determined to substitute for it a vertical polygon, composed of what have been improperly called *cylindric lenses*, but which in reality are rectilinear and horizontal prisms, distributing the light which they receive from the focus equally over the horizontal sector which they subtend. This polygon has a sufficient number of sides to enable it to give, at the angle formed by the junction of two of them, a light not very much inferior to what is produced by one of the sides; and upper and lower courses of curved mirrors are so placed as to make up for the deficiency of the light at the angles. The effect sought for in a fixed light is thus obtained in a much more perfect manner than by any combination of the parabolic mirrors formerly used in the British lighthouses.

An ingenious modification of the fixed apparatus is due

to the inventive mind of Fresnel, who conceived the happy idea of placing one apparatus of this kind in front of another, with the axes of the cylindric pieces crossing each other at right angles. As these cylindric pieces have the property of refracting all the rays which they receive from the focus into a direction perpendicular to the mixtilinear section which generates them, it is obvious that, if two refracting media of this sort be arranged as proposed by Fresnel, their joint action will unite the rays which come from their common focus into a beam, whose sectional area is equal to the overlapped surface of the two instruments, and thus produce the effect of an annular lens. It was by availing himself of this property of crossed prisms that Fresnel invented the distinction for lights, which he calls *a fixed light varied by flashes*; in which the flashes are caused by the revolution of cylindric media, with vertical axes round the fixed-light apparatus already described.

The modification just described is shown at fig. 16. This instrument is, however, now supplanted by a revolving apparatus, consisting of alternate sections of a fixed light apparatus, and a Holophotal apparatus to be afterwards described. By the revolution of this composite apparatus the same effect is obtained, while the flash is produced by the action of a *single* optical agent, instead of by two, as in Fresnel's arrangement.

Fresnel immediately perceived the necessity of combining, with the dioptric instruments which he had invented, a burner capable of producing a large volume of flame; and the rapidity with which he matured his notions on this subject, and at once produced an instrument admirably adapted for the end he had in view, affords one of the many proofs of that happy union of practical with theoretical talent for which he was so distinguished. Fresnel himself has modestly attributed much of the merit of the invention of this lamp to M. Arago; but that gentleman, with great candour, gives the whole credit to his deceased friend, in a notice regarding lighthouses, which appeared in the *Annuaire du Bureau des Longitudes* of 1831. The lamp has four concentric burners, which are defended from the action of the excessive heat produced by their united flames by means of a superabundant supply of oil which is thrown up from the cistern below by a clock-work movement, and constantly overflows the wicks, as in the mechanical lamp of Carcel. A very tall chimney is found to be necessary, in order to supply fresh currents of air to each wick with sufficient rapidity to support the combustion. The carbonization of the wicks, however, is by no means so rapid as might be expected, and it is even found that, after they have suffered a good deal, the flame is not sensibly diminished, as the great heat evolved from the mass of flame promotes the rising of the oil in the cotton. So perfect, indeed, is the action of this great lamp, that it has been known to burn for upwards of twelve hours without being snuffed, or even having the wicks raised.

The annexed diagrams will give a more perfect idea of the nature of the concentric burner than can easily be conveyed by words alone.

Fig. 13 shows a plan of a burner of four concentric wicks. The intervals which separate the wicks from each other, and allow the currents of air to pass, diminish in width a little as

Fig. 13.

they recede from the centre. Fig. 14 shows a section of this burner. C, C', C'', C''' are the rack handles for raising or depressing each wick. AB is the horizontal duct which leads the oil to the four wicks; L, L, L, are small plates of tin by which the burners are soldered to each other, and which are so placed as not to hinder the free passage of the air; P is a clamping screw which keeps at the proper height the gallery R, R which carries the chimney. Fig. 15 shows the burner with its glass chimney and damper. E is the glass chimney, F is a sheet-iron cylinder, which serves to give it a greater length, and has a small damper D, capable of being turned by a handle for regulating the supply of air; and B is the pipe which supplies the oil to the wicks. The great risk in using this lamp arises from the leather valves, that force the oil by a clock-work movement, being occasionally liable to derangement; and several of the lights on the French coast, and more especially the Corduan, have been extinguished for a few minutes by the failure of the lamp, an accident which has never, and scarcely can happen with the fountain lamps which illuminate the reflectors. To prevent the occurrence of such accidents, and to render their consequences less serious, various precautions have been resorted to. Amongst others, an alarum is attached to the lamp, consisting of a small cup pierced in the bottom, which receives part of the overflowing oil from the wicks, and is capable, when full, of balancing a weight placed at the opposite end of a lever. The moment the machinery stops, the cup ceases to receive the supply of oil, and the remainder running out at the bottom, the equilibrium of the lever is destroyed, and, in falling, it disengages a spring which rings a bell sufficiently loud to waken the keeper, should he chance to be asleep. There is another precaution of more importance, which consists in having always at hand in the lightroom a spare lamp trimmed and adjusted to the height for the focus, which may be substituted for the other in case of accident. It ought to be noticed, however, that it takes about twenty minutes from the time of applying the light to the wicks to bring the flame to its full strength, which, in order to produce its best effect, should stand at the height of nearly four inches (10cm). The inconveniences attending this lamp have led to several attempts to improve it; and amongst others M. Delaveleye has proposed to substitute a pump having a metallic piston, in place of the leather valves, which require constant care, and must be frequently renewed. A lamp was constructed in this manner by M. Lepaute, and tried at Corduan; but it was afterwards discontinued until some further improvements could be made upon it. It has lately been much improved by M. Wagner, an ingenious artist whom M. Fresnel employed to carry some of his improvements into effect. In the dioptric lights on the Scotch coast, a common lamp with

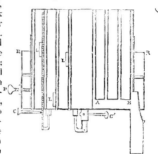

Fig. 14.

Light-
houses
a large wick is kept constantly ready for lighting, and in the event of the sudden extinction of the mechanical lamp by the failure of the valves, it is only necessary to unscrew and remove its burner, and put the reserve-lamp in its place. The height of this lamp is so arranged, that its flame is in the focus of the lenses, when the lamp is placed on the ring which supports the burner of the mechanical lamp, and as its flame, though not very brilliant, has a considerable volume, it will answer the purpose of maintaining the light for an hour or two until the light-keepers have time to repair the valves of the mechanical lamp.

Divergence
of the an-
nular
lenses
The divergence of the annular lens is greatly less than that of the parabolic mirror. It may be estimated in the following manner. Let Δ be the angle of divergence of any ray emerging from the lens, l the distance of the point of incidence from the principal focus of the lens, and r the radius of the flame, and we have $\sin \Delta = \dfrac{r}{l}$, and when Δ' is made the angle of the effective divergence of the lens, we have $\Delta' = 2\Delta$.

Adopting this rule we find the effective divergence of the lens to be about $5° 9'$, which does not differ much from the observed divergence.

Manufac-
ture of di-
optric in-
struments
The manufacture of the dioptric instruments is not distinguished by any peculiarity which requires special notice, the grinding and polishing being performed by means of powders gradually increasing in fineness, successively applied as in the ordinary process of grinding glass. The zones are united by a glue which possesses the important property of being able to resist the action of considerable heat, whilst it is by no means brittle. M Fresnel intrusted the work of building the first lens to the late M Soleil, optician to the king of France, to whose zeal and intelligence he bears ample testimony in the *Memoire*, in which he describes the invention.

Testing of
lenses
In order to test the figure of the lenses, moulds carefully made may be applied, or the lens being mounted on a stand which permits its being set at any angle, the accuracy of the whole instrument, and of each portion of it, may be separately tested by the form and size of the spectrum which is formed in the principal focus, by permitting the solar rays to fall upon the lens at right angles. When any particular portion is to be tried, the rest of the surface is covered with discs of strong grey paper or pasteboard. Another method may be employed similar to that already described as applicable to reflectors. This method consists in finding whether a small object placed in any point of the axis farther from the lens than the principal focus, has its image refracted accurately to a point on a screen placed in the conjugate focus which is due to that distance. The same principle of testing the instrument is also applied when a person stationed at a given short distance in front of the lens observes whether its whole surface be completely illuminated by a small flame placed in the conjugate focus corresponding to that distance. All that is necessary, therefore, is to determine these distances by means of formulæ which express the relations of the distances of the object and its image. If δ represent the distance of the eye from the lens, ϕ the principal focus, and ϕ' the distance of the conjugate focus corresponding to the observer's distance δ, then we have $\phi' = \dfrac{\delta\phi}{\delta - \phi}$.

If again adopting the same notation, we wish to find the distance at which the image of an object placed at a given distance from the lens greater than that of the principal focus, should be accurately impressed on a screen, we have $\delta = \dfrac{\phi\phi'}{\phi' - \phi}$

Curved
mirrors
The curved mirror placed above and below the lenses as a supplement to them are strictly speaking constituted by portions of parabolic having their foci coincident with

the common flame of the system. In practice, however, they are made portions of a curve surface, ground by the radius of the circle which osculates the given parabola, and passes tangentially through the middle of the chord which subtends the arc of the mirror. These mirrors are plates of glass, silvered on the back, and set in flat cases of sheet brass. They are suspended on a circular frame of screws, which are attached to the backs of the cases, and which afford the means of adjusting them to their true position in the light-room, so that they may reflect the horizon of the lighthouse to an observer's eye placed in the focus of the system. In order to test the accuracy of the mirrors, recourse may again be had to the formulæ of conjugate foci, thus, if we put r equal to the radius of curvature of the mirror, d equal to the given distance of any object from the mirror, and d' equal to the distance of a moveable screen, which shall receive the true image of the object if the mirror be accurately formed, we shall have for this latter distance $d' = \dfrac{rd}{2d - r}$

Power of
the annular
lenses, cy-
lindric re-
fractors
and curved
mirrors
The effect of an annular lens may be estimated at moderate distances to be nearly equal to that of 3000 Argand flames of about an inch diameter, that of a cylindric refractor at about 250, and that of a curved mirror may, perhaps, on an average, be assumed at about 10 Argand flames.

Catadiop-
tric light
A beautiful apparatus, which has received the name of the *catadioptric* light, from the compound action by which it is characterized, was another of Fresnel's applications of dioptric instruments to the purposes of a lighthouse. This elegant apparatus consists of thirteen rings of glass of various diameters, arranged one above another, in an oval form. The five middle rings have an interior diameter of 11.81 inches (30^{cm}), and form a cylindric lens, similar to that already described under the head "cylindric refractors." The other rings or prisms, five of which are upper and three lower, are ground and set in such a manner that they project all the light derived from the focus in a direction parallel to the other rays by *total reflection*. This effect is produced by arranging the prisms, so that the incident rays, after being refracted at the first surface, shall strike the second side of the prism at such an angle that, instead of passing through the prism at that point, they shall be *totally reflected* from it, and, after a second refraction, emerge from the third side in a direction parallel to those transmitted by the middle or simply refracting rings. When this apparatus is employed to light only a part of the horizon, the rings are discontinued on the side next to the land and room is thus obtained for using a common fountain lamp, but when the whole horizon is to be illuminated, the apparatus must inclose the flame on every side, so that it has in this case been found necessary to employ the hydrostatic lamp of Thilorier in which the balance is sulphate of zinc in solution. Fresnel was prevented, by an early death, the consequence of severe application to scientific pursuits, from ever constructing this beautiful instrument, and it was reserved for the present enlightened secretary of the *Commission des Phares* to complete his brother's invention.

The nature of this apparatus will be fully understood by a reference to fig. 16, which shows its section and plan. Γ is the focal point in which the flame is placed, r, r cylindrical refractors, forming by their union a cylinder with a lamp in its axis, and producing a zone of light of equal intensity all round the horizon, and r', r' are cylindric refractors having their axes at right angles to those of the refractors r, r, and revolving round them. These exterior refractors in front of the inner refractors, which have, as already described under the head of cylindric Refractors, produce by compound refraction, a beam similar to that resulting from an annular lens. r, r

are catadioptric prismatic rings acting by *total reflection*, and giving out zones of light of equal intensity at every point of the horizon The dotted lines show the course traversed by the rays of light which proceed from the lamp and are acted upon by the rings of glass The catadioptric rings supply the places of the curved mirrors, which had at one time to be employed in the larger class of lights for a similar purpose, and as the reflection from the inner surface of a prism is, theoretically speak-

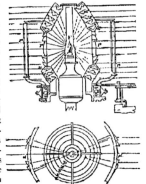

Fig 10

ing, *total*, and the whole loss of light is merely that which is due to absorption in passing through the glass, and that which takes place at the two surfaces there must of necessity be a much greater proportion of the incident light transmitted by the catadioptric action than can ever be obtained from the most perfect reflecting surface, the loss from reflection being held to be in no case less than one-half of the incident light

The loss of light by reflection at the surface of the most perfect mirrors, and the perishable nature of the material composing their polish, induced Mr Alan Stevenson, so far back as 1835, in a report on the Light of Inchkeith, which had just been altered to the dioptric system, to propose the substitution of *totally reflecting* prisms, even in lights of the first order or largest dimensions. In this attempt he was much encouraged by the singular liberality of M Léonor Fresnel, who not only freely communicated the method pursued by his distinguished brother Augustin Fresnel, in determining the forms of the zones of the small apparatus, introduced by him into the Harbour Lights of France, and his own mode of rigorously solving some of the preliminary questions involved in the computations ; but also made various important suggestions, which substantially embrace the whole subject The result was the preparation of a table containing Mr Stevenson's calculations of the forms of the zones of the first order, which are verifications of those of M Fresnel, and the first catadioptric apparatus ever constructed, through the ardour and perseverance of M François Soleil, on so magnificent a scale, was fitted up in the Skerryvore Lighthouse In December 1843, a trial of the apparatus, attended with complete success, was made at the Royal Observatory of Paris, whereby it appeared that the illuminating effect of the cupola of zones was to that of the seven upper tiers of mirrors of the first order, as 140 to 87

The cylin-
dric form
given to the
refracting
belts of the
first order

Mr Alan Stevenson having been directed by the Commissioners of the Northern Lighthouses to convert the fixed catoptric light of the Isle of May into a dioptric light of the first order, proposed that an attempt should be made to form a true cylindric, instead of a polygonal belt, for the refracting part of the apparatus, and this task was successfully completed by Messrs Cookson of Newcastle The defect of the polygon lies in the excess of the radius of the circumscribing circle over that of the inscribed circle, which occasions an unequal distribution of light between its angles and the centre of each of its sides; and this fault

can only be fully remedied by constructing a cylindric belt, whose generating line is the middle rectilineal section of an *annular* lens, revolving about a vertical axis passing through the principal focus. This is, in fact, the only form which can possibly produce an equal diffusion of the incident light over every part of the horizon

In a report to the Commissioners of the Northern Lights there is the following description of the refractors constructed for the Isle of May light.—"I at first imagined," says Mr Alan Stevenson, "that the whole hoop of refractors might be built between two metallic rings, connecting them to each other solely by the means employed in cementing the pieces of the annular lenses, but a little consideration convinced me that this construction would make it necessary to build the zone at the lighthouse itself, and would thus greatly increase the risk of fracture I was therefore reluctantly induced to divide the whole cylinder into ten arcs, each of which being set in a metallic frame, might be capable of being moved separately The chance of any error in the figure of the instrument has thus a probability of being confined within narrower limits, whilst the rectification of any defective part becomes at the same time more easy One other variation from the mode of construction at first contemplated has been forced upon me by the repeated failures which occurred in attempting to form the middle zone in one piece, and it was at length found necessary to divide this belt by a line passing through the horizontal plane of the focus This division of the central zone, however, is attended with no appreciable loss of light, as the entire coincidence of the junction of the two pieces with the horizontal plane of the focus, confines the interception of the light to the fine joint at which they are cemented With the exception of these trifling changes, the idea at first entertained of the construction of this instrument was fully realized, at the very first attempt, in the manufactory of Messrs Cookson" At a subsequent period the central zones were formed in one piece and the arrangement of the apparatus greatly improved, by giving to the metallic frames which contain the prisms a rhomboidal instead of a rectangular form The junction of the frames being thus inclined from the perpendicular, do not in any azimuth intercept the light throughout the whole height of the refracting belt, but the interception is confined to a small rhomboidal space, whose area is inversely proportional to the sine of the angle of inclination; and when the helical joints are formed between the opposite angles of the rectangular frames, the amount of intercepted light becomes absolutely equal in every azimuth Time and perseverance, and the patience and skill of M François Soleil, who was urged to undertake the task, was at length crowned with success, and Mr Stevenson had the satisfaction of at last seeing a fixed light apparatus, of a truly cylindric form, with its central belt in one piece and the joints of each panel inclined to the horizon at such an angle as to render the light perfectly equal in every azimuth Lanterns with diagonal framings are now also constructed in conformity with this arrangement of the zones

The change of the light at the Isle of May, from the catoptric to the dioptric system, was generally acknowledged to be an improvement A committee of the Royal Society of Edinburgh made some observations on the two lights which were exhibited in contrast on the night of the 26th of October 1836, from the town of Dunbar, which is distant about 13 miles from the lighthouse Their report, which was drawn up by Professor Forbes, concludes in these words —

"The following conclusions seem to be warranted .—

---

1 "The form e all n   ab rh m   l,   t u ld ap   n of a l   u nt e t l b n two   utting the enveloped cylind r at right   l

"1. That at a distance of 13 miles, the mean effect of the new light is very much superior to the mean effect of the old light (perhaps in the ratio of two to one).

"2. That at *all* distances, the new light has a prodigious superiority to the old, from the equality of its effects in all azimuths.

"3. That the new light fulfils rigorously the conditions required for the distribution of light to the greatest advantage.

"4. That at distances much exceeding 13 miles, the new light must still be a very effective one, though to what extent the committee have not observed. The light is understood to be still a good one, when seen from Edinburgh at a distance of about 30 miles."

There are few finer specimens of art than an entire apparatus for a fixed light of the first order, as shown in fig. 17. It consists of a central belt of refractors, forming a hollow cylinder 6 feet in diameter, and 30 inches high; below it are six triangular rings of glass, ranged in a cylindrical form, and above a crown of thirteen rings of glass, forming by their union a hollow cage, composed of polished glass, 10 feet high and 6 feet in diameter! There is no work of art more beautiful or more creditable to the boldness, intelligence, and zeal of the artist.

Fig. 17.

All the lights on the dioptric principle are illuminated by a flame placed in the centre of the apparatus or common focus of the principal lenses and cylindric refractors which are ranged round it. The burner of the lamp varies in its dimensions and its consumption of oil, according to the size of the instruments employed, which also determines what is called the *order* of the light, a name expressive of its *power* and *range*. Above and below the strictly dioptric part of the apparatus of each order there are also accessory parts, which, as just described, and shown in fig. 17, consist in fixed lights of catadioptric prisms arranged in tiers, one above another, like the leaves of a Venetian blind, and placed so as to reflect to the horizon the rays received from the lamp, which is in their common focus. In all revolving lights, up till 1850, the apparatus above the principal lenses either consisted of prisms similar to those described for fixed lights, or was diacatoptric, being composed of an union of eight lenses of 19·68 inches (50ᶜᵐ) of focal distance, inclined inwards to the flame, which is in their common focus, and thus forming a frustum of an octagonal pyramid of 50° of inclination. These upper lenses were surmounted by plane mirrors, placed so as to reflect horizontally the beams transmitted by the lenses. In placing these upper lenses, it has been thought advisable to give their axes a horizontal inclination of 7° from that of the great lenses. By this arrangement, the flash of the upper lenses always precedes that of the principal lenses.

The use of the accessory apparatus is to collect the rays, which would otherwise pass above and below the main lenses, without contributing to the brilliancy of the light. These inclined mirrors and lenses have, since 1850, been entirely laid aside on the introduction of the Holophotal system of revolving lights, to be afterwards explained, in which totally reflecting prisms form part of the *revolving* apparatus, and supersede the inclined mirrors and lenses. The nature of the whole revolving apparatus of Fresnel will be more fully understood by referring to fig. 18, which is a section

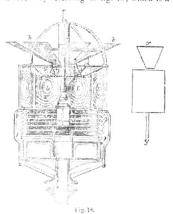

Fig. 18.

of a revolving dioptric apparatus of the first order; L, L, are the great annular lenses, forming by their union an octagonal prism, with the lamp in its axis, and projecting in horizontal beams the light which they receive from the focus; a, a, upper lenses, forming by their union a frustum of an octagonal pyramid of 50° of inclination, and having their foci coinciding in the focal point. They parallelize the rays of light which pass over the lenses. b, b, plane mirrors, placed above the pyramidal lenses, and so inclined as to project the beams reflected from them in planes parallel to the horizon.

The dioptric lights used in France are divided into four orders, in relation to their power and range; but in regard to their characteristic appearances, this division does not apply, as, in each of the orders, lights of identically the same character may be found, differing only in the distance at which they can be seen, and in the expense of their maintenance. The four orders may be briefly described as follows:—

1*st*. Lights of the first order, having an interior radius or focal distance of 36·22 inches (92ᶜᵐ), and lighted by a lamp of four concentric wicks, consuming 570½ gallons of oil per annum.

2*d*. Lights of the second order, having an interior radius of 27·55 inches (70ᶜᵐ), lighted by a lamp of three concentric wicks, consuming 384 gallons of oil per annum.

3*d*. Lights of the third order, lighted by a lamp of two concentric wicks, consuming 183 gallons of oil per annum. The instruments used in these lights are of two kinds, one having a focal distance of 19·68 inches (50ᶜᵐ), and the other of 9·84 inches (25ᶜᵐ).

4*th*. Lights of the fourth order, or harbour lights, having an internal radius of 5·9 inches (15ᶜᵐ), and lighted by a lamp of one wick, or Argand burner, consuming 48 gallons of oil per annum.

The great loss of light by natural divergence in the parabolic reflector, and the separation of the rays into as many portions as there are lenses in the flame, in Fresnel's re-volving dioptric apparatus, together with the objectionable plan for intercepting the rays which pass above and below the lenses, led Mr Thomas Stevenson to inquire into the possibility of increasing the intensity of lights by changes in the optical arrangements. The parabolic reflectors act chiefly on the *posterior* portion of the flame, and generally receive about $\frac{3}{4}$ths of the whole luminous sphere, while a series of dioptric instruments can affect only an *anterior cone*, amounting to about $\frac{2}{5}$ths. Certain deductions, due to the form of the flame and the loss by reflection and re-fraction, reduce these numbers to $\frac{1}{2}$d for the reflectors, and $\frac{7}{20}$ths for the lenses, as the amount of light actually given forth by each system. Both arrangements are, therefore, so far unsuitable for revolving lights, in which the concentration of all the diverging rays into pencils of parallel rays is the grand object to be aimed at. The pro-blem which Mr Stevenson assigned to himself was to *pro-duce the brightest beam from a given flame by the smallest number of reflections and refractions.* This object he at-tained partly by combining dioptric with catoptric and catadioptric action, and partly by an *extension* of the *lenti-cular action itself over a greater subtense.* To this arrange-ment the name of *Holophotal* has been given, to signify the useful application of the *whole* of the light.

One mode of producing this effect is to combine an an-

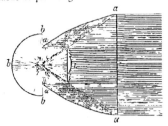

Fig 19

nular lens L, figs 19 and 20, a parabolic conoid a, trun-cated at its parameter, and hemispherical mirror b. The lens, when at its proper focal distance from the flame, subtends the same angle from it as the outer lips of the paraboloid. The hemi-spherical reflector occupies the place of the parabolic conoid which has been cut off behind the parameter. The flame is at once in the centre of the hemispherical mirror and in the common focus of the lens and paraboloid.

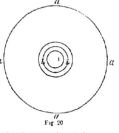

Fig 20

Suppose the whole sphere of rays emanating from the flame to be divided into two por-tions, viz., the hemisphere of front rays and the hemisphere of back rays. Part of the anterior hemisphere of rays is inter-cepted by the lens and made parallel by its action, while the remainder is intercepted by the paraboloidal surface, and made parallel by its action. The rays forming the posterior hemisphere, and which fall upon the hemispherical reflector, are sent back through the focus in the same lines, but in direc-tions opposite to those in which they came, whence passing onwards they are in part refracted by the lens, while the rest are made parallel by the paraboloid. The back rays thus finally emerge horizontally in union with the light from the anterior hemisphere. This instrument, therefore, fulfils the conditions prescribed, by collecting the *entire sphere of di-verging rays into one parallel beam of light.*

The first instrument constructed upon this principle was for the North Harbour of Peterhead, where it has been in use since August 1849. Mr A. Stevenson has also adopted an instrument of this kind, on a large scale, in Hoy Sound Lighthouse, one of the Northern Lights' stations.

Experiments were lately made at Gullan Hill to test the comparative power of an instrument on this principle (the reflecting part being of brass and but roughly finished), and a highly-finished silver reflector of the usual construc-tion, both instruments being 25 inches in diameter at the lips. The lights were viewed at distances of from 7 to 12 miles every night during a week, and in every instance the brass reflector on the holophotal principle had the advantage of the silver reflector, and on one occasion, when the atmo-sphere was thick, the light from the holophotal brass re-flector was alone visible.

In so far as concerns the arrangement of the different parts, irrespective of the nature of the materials of which they are composed, the light emitted from any given flame by the instruments just described, should be the light of *maximum intensity.* But the most accurate experiments which have been undertaken by scientific observers have shown that reflection from the best silvered mirrors, and even from metallic specula made with the utmost care for experimental purposes, involves a loss of light by ab-sorption of not less than about one-half of the whole in-cident rays.

The advantage of employing as largely as possible the principle of *total reflection* from glass in place of ordinary reflection from metallic specula, induced Mr T. Stevenson to attempt further improvements in the holophotal system of illumination. If we retain the lens and the spherical mirror of the holophotal apparatus just described, and, in place of the paraboloid, conceive the arc between the lens and the spherical mirror to be filled up with glass rings, which are the solids of revolution generated by the rotation of the cross section of the totally reflecting prisms used in fixed lights, round a horizontal axis passing through the flame, we shall then have *extended the action of the lens, so as to parallelize one-half of the whole sphere of incident rays.* Such an arrangement is shown in figs. 21 and 22, where L

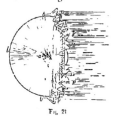

Fig 21

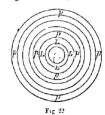

Fig 22

is the lens, p the totally reflecting prisms, and b is the spherical mirror. The distinguishing peculiarity of this arrangement is, that the prisms, instead of transmitting the light in parallel vertical plates, diverging all round as in the fixed light apparatus of Fresnel, produce an extension of the lenticular or *quaquaversal* action of the common an-nular lens, by assembling the light around its axis in the form of concentric hollow cylinders. In order to distinguish this system of prisms from those introduced by M. Fresnel, which have no lenticular action, they may therefore be termed *catadioptric lenses.*

The writer of this article has lately heard, that, although it had never been proposed to use such prisms for lighthouse purposes, a small lamp, for lighting the quays of a canal in Paris, was made by M. A. Fresnel, in 1825, in which some prisms similar to the above described, form an accessory part, but no drawing or description of such an apparatus was ever published. It is also said that [...] seems to have been lost till Mr T. Stevenson described his plan in 1849. Since that time, thirty-six instruments have been made at Edinburgh, on the small scale, both for home and foreign use. The first instance in which these prisms were ever applied to lighthouses was at the Hor-burgh Light, near Singapore, the optical part of which was designed by Mr T. Stevenson. This was the first time that the principle of total reflection was applied to the moving apparatus of revolving lights. The first light of the large order, on this principle, was constructed under the direction of Mr Alan Stevenson, for North Ronaldsay, in the Orkneys; and seven others have recently been made in Paris for French and American lighthouses. There can be no doubt that this arrangement will be generally adopted, instead of the combination of inclined lenses and plane mirrors, first employed at Corduan, and subsequently in other revolving lights in France and Britain.

By an elegant adaptation of *totally reflecting zones*, Mr Thomas Stevenson has further succeeded in substituting, for a reflector of metal or silvered glass, a *polyzonal totally reflecting hemisphere of glass* (*vide* fig. 5). By this arrangement, reflection from metallic specula is abolished from every part of the system, and the principles of total reflection and simple refraction alone are employed.

The action of these glass zones will be best understood by referring to fig. 23, which gives the cross section of one

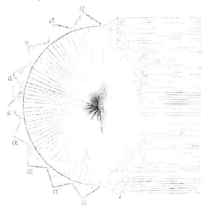

Fig. 23.

of them; f shows the flame or centre of the system, and the diverging rays are represented by dotted lines, the arrows indicating the direction of a ray before and after being altered by the prism. The side bc is concave, the centre of curvature being in f, the centre of the flame. The surfaces of the other sides, ab, and ac, are portions of parabolas, whose common focus is f, or of circles osculating the parabolic curves. These parabolic surfaces face each other, and their tangents form an angle of 99° with each other at the vertex of the prism. Any ray proceeding from the centre f will be received as a normal to the surface bc, and will consequently pass on without suffering any deviation at c, where it meets the prism, to its incidence on the surface ab, where

it will be tot
the sphere a...

total reflection, and finally emerges in a radial direction without deviation at the point e. An exactly similar action will take place simultaneously with another ray in the same path from the flame, though passing in an opposite direction. The concentric zones, a, which compose the dome (*vide* fig. 24), are solids of revolution, generated by the rotation round the horizontal axis of the instrument of triangles similar to a, b, c (fig. 23), with a radius equal to af. The angle formed by the radius with the horizontal axis of the instrument varies from nearly 90° down to zero, as shown in fig. 24. Where these angles vanish at a', a conoid will result, having the radius of its base equal to the semichord of its inner surface. It will be seen that the prisms b, a, c, fig. 23, resemble in their action that of the drops of rain which give rise to the phenomenon of the *secondary* rainbow. In fig. 24, which shows the whole instrument complete, L represents the common lens acting on the rays by refraction only; p, the catadioptric portion of the lens acting by refraction and total reflection; and a, a', a, the prisms acting by total reflection only. Part of a hemispherical dome on this principle has now been successfully executed.

Fig. 25 shows the adaptation of the holophotal system to Fresnel's revolving light of the first order. L, L are the lenses, and p, p the catadioptric lenticular rings. The advantage of this system will clearly appear by comparing it with Fresnel's apparatus (fig. 18). At each of figs. 25 and 18, diagrams marked x y show proportionate sections of the beam of light given out by the two arrangements respectively. The objection-

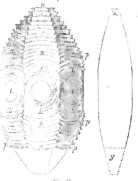

Fig. 25.

able arrangement of the lenses and mirrors a and b (fig. 18), in which so much of the light is lost, by the introduction of so many surfaces, and is also superseded.

For pointing out sunken reefs, on which no lighthouse can be placed, two plans have been proposed by Mr Thomas Stevenson. The first, or *dipping* light, consists in throwing a pencil of rays from a lantern on shore *down* upon the reef, by inclining the vertical axis of the apparatus at the requisite angle; and by this arrangement the visibility of the light is confined within certain limits, the passing within which is, to the seaman, a sign of danger, and a warning to *haul off* seaward. The second, or *apparent* light, applies to reefs on which a small beacon, capable of bearing a cage on its top, can be built, but which affords no room for a lighthouse tower. In this cage is placed some *reflecting* apparatus, either wholly *catadioptric*, or combining a *plane mirror* with a vertical system of straight lenticular prisms; and upon this there is projected, from a lantern on shore, a beam of light, which is diverted (according to the angle at which the cage apparatus on the beacon is set) into any given direction that may be required. This latter plan has been most successfully applied to the entrance of Stornoway Loch, a much-used harbour of refuge in the Lewis, and has drawn from many shipmasters frequenting that port written expressions of their satisfaction with the light, which is well seen *a mile and a half* in the offing; a distance amply sufficient for the limited purposes for which such lights should be used. The name *apparent* is given to this

a flame on
the rock.
a, which are

Adaptation
of the Ho-
lophotal
system to
Fresnel's
Apparatus.

Light-
houses

lolophotal mirror
condensers
or illumi-
ating nar-
ow sounds

not required to show all round the horizon, the light of the darkened part is either allowed to be lost, or is returned through the focus by means of a portion of a spherical mirror   There are, however, cases frequently occurring to the lighthouse engineer where it would be very desirable to employ this spare light, not in the direction diametrically opposite to the darkened arc, but in some other direction more suited to the configuration of the coast   The apparatus for Isle Oronsay of which fig 26 is a horizontal section through

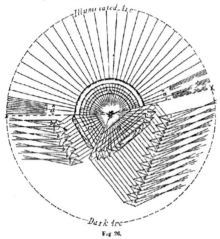

Fig 26.

the focus, is the first which has been designed with a view to the most advantageous employment of this spare light

The lighthouse of Isle Oronsay is situate in the narrow Sound of Skye, and, throughout nearly the whole of the illuminated arc, does not require to be seen to a greater distance than 3 or 4 miles, while in one direction (down the sound) it can be seen for 15 miles, and in another (up the sound) it can be seen for about 7 miles   If, therefore, a light were erected sufficiently powerful to be seen at the greatest distance required, it must be very greatly too powerful in every other direction, and consequently there would be a great waste of oil , while, if an apparatus only powerful enough for the short range were employed, it would become necessary to make use of subsidiary apparatus, implying additional lamps, and an increased expenditure of oil, to show up and down the sound   The apparatus shown was designed by Mr I Stevenson, with the view of reinforcing the ordinary fixed-light apparatus in the directions of greatest range   This is effected by distributing in these directions the spare light on the dark side of the lantern, which, if returned through the focus in the ordinary manner by means of a spherical mirror, would only tend to strengthen that portion of the light which is already sufficiently powerful

A is 167° of a small fixed-light apparatus subtending the entire arc to be illuminated , so that all the rest of the light, or 193°, is spare light   Of this, 129° are parallelized by the holophotal apparatus B , and the rays, falling on a series of equal and similar prisms, a, are again refracted, but in the horizontal plane only , and after passing through a focal point (independent for each prism), emerge in a series of twelve equal and parallel beams, having a divergence of about 10°, which are also equal and parallel to the diverging beam, a, and, consequently, according to well known optical laws, have the effect of strengthening it as much as if they were actually superimposed upon it   As the light of 139 is, in this manner, condensed into about 10 , the effect must be from 12 to 14 times that of the unassisted apparatus, and

should, therefore, be amply sufficient for a range of 15 miles   In like manner, the light parallelized by the other holophote C, are refracted by the prisms b, so as to strengthen the arc β, which will thus be rendered amply powerful for a range of 7 miles   The greater number of rays in the arcs a and β are intended to indicate the additional density due to the action of the subsidiary prisms   We shall only add, that when arcs of coloured light are to be employed, this method of strengthening any particular portion of the light becomes very important, as offering a ready method of equalizing the general range, otherwise interfered with by the enormous absorption of coloured media, and we might suggest, that, even where the light requires to be shown all round, it is possible to supplement any arc at the expense of any other, by cutting off an ordinary apparatus by a horizontal plane at any suitable height, and mounting a portion of a holophote and a series of prisms above it   By a somewhat similar arrangement to what has been described for Oronsay, the whole of the rays proceeding from a plane may be spread over any desired arc of the horizon.

General remarks

Having thus fully described the catoptric and dioptric systems of illumination, it might be expected that we should institute a comparison between them   This, however, may now be considered unnecessary, as the universal adoption of the dioptric system speaks for itself   Its advantages are indeed too numerous and too palpable to be overlooked, combining, as they do, efficiency of action and fitness to meet every requirement, with economy in the consumption of oil , and we may safely say, that in all those countries where this important branch of administration is conducted with the care and solicitude which it deserves, the dioptric system has been adopted to the complete exclusion of the catoptric, except, indeed, in certain cases where economy of first construction and simplicity of detail are objects of primary importance

To the Dutch belongs the honour of having first, after the French, embraced the system of Fresnel in their lights   The Commissioners of the Northern Lights followed in the train of improvement, and, in 1834, sent Mr Alan Stevenson on a mission to Paris, with full power to take such steps for acquiring a perfect knowledge of the dioptric system, and forming an opinion on its merits, as he should find necessary   The singular liberality with which he was received by M Leonor Fresnel, brother of the late illustrious inventor of the system, and his successor as the Secretary of the Lighthouse Commission of France, afforded Mr A Stevenson the means of making such a report on his return as induced the Commissioners to authorize him to remove the reflecting apparatus of the revolving light at Inchkeith, and substitute dioptric instruments in its place   This change was completed, and the light exhibited on the evening of 1st October 1835 , and so great was the satisfaction which the change produced, that the Commissioners immediately instructed Mr Stevenson to make a similar change at the fixed light of the Isle of May, where the new light was exhibited on the 22d September 1836.   The Trinity House of London followed next in adopting the improved system, and employed Mr A Stevenson to superintend the construction of a revolving dioptric light of the first order, which was afterwards erected at the Start Point in Devonshire   Other countries followed, and the Report of the Lighthouse Board of America, published in 1852, which recommends (p 13) the adoption of Fresnel's dioptric system, and the holophotal improvements, is a very full body of information on lighthouse subjects, extending over about 750 pages   Even Turkey has followed in the train of improvement, and we believe that a light on the dioptric principle will shortly be exhibited (if it be not already completed) from the Isle of Serpents   Fresnel, who is already classed with the greatest of those inventive minds which extend the boundaries of human knowledge, will thus, at the same

Light-
houses

Light-
houses

time, receive a place amongst those benefactors of the species who have consecrated their genius to the common good of mankind; and, wherever maritime intercourse prevails, the solid advantages which his labours have procured will be felt and acknowledged

When, however, this system was in its infancy, there were several objections raised to its adoption, which appeared to be of very considerable importance, though the experience of years has proved that they are not insurmountable. The first, and probably the most important, was the liability of the lamp to be extinguished from the failure of the leather work of the oil-pumps—a most serious objection, inasmuch as, from there being only one lamp, its failure implies the extinction of the light. The means adopted to remedy this have been already described (vide " mechanical lamp"), and an experience of twenty-one years in the Northern Lighthouses has proved them to be sufficient for the purpose; for during the whole of that time (although it has on several occasions been necessary to light the spare lamp) the light has only on one occasion been totally extinguished, a casualty which was caused by the keeper sleeping on his watch

The only other objection worthy of mention is the short duration of the flash in revolving lights, owing to the small divergence ($5° 9$) of the annular lens. This has been corrected by setting the inclined mirrors, or holophotal prisms, a little in advance of the great lenses, so that they precede, and consequently prolong, the principal flash. M. Degrand has also proposed to cut the whole apparatus by a horizontal plane passing through the focus, and to set one portion a few degrees in advance of the other, a plan which has considerable advantages, as all the portions of the beam are more nearly of equal intensity

Spherico-
cylindric
lenses.

Mr T Stevenson moreover, suggests an ingenious method of remedying this evil, by constructing lenses whose aberration in the vertical plane is corrected, while that in the horizontal plane may be adjusted to any determinate amount. In the application of this method of construction to the annular lenses they would be ground on the external surface as before, but the internal surface would be a portion of a vertical cylinder of suitable radius. Thus each vertical section would be similar to that of a plano-convex lens as at present, and would refract the rays accordingly, while the horizontal sections would be of a meniscal form, and would act only by the excess of their convexity over their concavity. Thus, by varying the radius of the cylinder, any amount of horizontal divergence may be obtained, and this without much increasing the thickness of the glass, at least in the case of revolving lights, in which a curve of long radius might be applied

Fuel of
light-
houses

The oil, until lately, most generally employed in the lighthouses of the United Kingdom was the sperm oil of commerce, which is obtained from the South Sea whale (*Physeter macrocephalus*). In France, the colza oil, which is expressed from the seed of a species of wild cabbage (*Brassica oleracea colza*) and the olive oil, are chiefly used, and a species of the former has now been successfully introduced into the British lighthouses

The advantages of the colza oil are thus stated by the engineer of the Scottish Lighthouse Board:—

" It appears from pretty careful photometrical measurements of various kinds, that the light derived from the colza oil is, in point of intensity, a little superior to that derived from the spermaceti oil, being in the ratio of 1·036 to 1. The colza oil burns both in the Fresnel lamp and the single Argand burner with a thick wick during seventeen hours, without requiring any snuffing of the wick or any adjustment of the damper, and the flame seems to be more steady
from sperma
to the great

of glass chimneys with the colza than with the spermaceti oil.

Light-
houses

The consumption of oil seems in the Fresnel lamp to be 121 for colza, and 114 for spermaceti; while in the common Argand, the consumption appears to be 910 for colza, and 902 for spermaceti; and if we assume the means of these numbers, 515 for colza, and 508 for spermaceti, as representing the relative expenditure of these oils; and if the price of colza be 3s 9d while that of spermaceti is 6s 9d per imperial gallon, we shall have a saving in the ratio of 1 to 1·755, which, at the present rate of supply for the Northern Lights, would give a saving of about L.3266 per annum "

Gas

In a few lighthouses which are near towns, the gas of pit coal has been used, and there are certain advantages, more especially in dioptric lights, where there is only one large central flame, which would render the use of gas desirable. The form of the flame, which is an object of considerable importance, would thus be rendered less variable, and could be more easily regulated, and the inconvenience of the clock-work of the lamp would be wholly avoided. But it is obvious that gas is by no means suitable for the majority of lighthouses, their distant situation, and generally difficult access, rendering the transport of large quantities of coal expensive and uncertain, whilst in many of them there is no means of erecting the apparatus necessary for manufacturing gas. There are other considerations which must induce us to pause before adopting gas as the fuel of lighthouses; for, however much the risk of accident may be diminished in the present day, it still forms a question, which ought not to be hastily decided, how far we should be justified in running even the most remote risk of explosion in establishments such as lighthouses, the sudden failure of which might involve consequences of the most fatal description, and the situation of which is often such, that their re-establishment must be a work of great expense and time

Drummond
and Voltaic
lights

The application of the Drummond and Voltaic lights to lighthouse purposes is, owing to their prodigious intensity, a very desirable consummation, but it is surrounded by so many practical difficulties, that it may, in the present state of our knowledge, be pronounced unattainable. The uncertainty which attends the exhibition of both these lights is of itself a sufficient reason for coming to this conclusion. But other reasons unhappily are not wanting. The smallness of the flame renders those lights wholly inapplicable to dioptric instruments, which require a great body of flame, in order to produce a degree of divergence sufficient to render the duration of the flash in revolving lights long enough to answer the purpose of the manner. M Fresnel made some experiments on the application of the Drummond light to dioptric instruments, which completely demonstrate their unfitness for this combination. He found that the light obtained by placing it in the focus of a great annular lens was much more intense than that produced by the great lamp and lens of Corduan; but the divergence did not exceed 30', so that, in a revolution like that of Corduan, the flashes would last only 1½ second, and would not, therefore, be seen in such a manner as to suit the practical purposes of a revolving light. The great cylindric refractor, used in fixed lights of the first order, was also tried with the Drummond light in its focus, but it gave coloured spectra at the top and bottom and only a small bar of white light was transmitted from the centre of the instrument. The same deficiency of divergence completely unfits the combination of the Drummond light with the reflector for the purposes of a fixed light, and even if this cause did not operate against its application in revolving lights on the catoptric plan, the supply of the gases, which is attended with almost insurmountable difficulties,
of the light
st regarding

General
questions
regarding
lighthouses

Distinction
and distri-
bution of
lights

lighthouses, which appear to open an extensive field of inquiry, and it may be doubted whether some of them have received that degree of consideration to which their importance entitles them. Amongst these we may rank the numerous questions which may be raised regarding the most effective kind of distinctions for lights. Those distinctions may be naturally expected to be the most effective which strike an observer by their *appearance* alone. Thus a red and white light, a revolving and a fixed light, offer *appearances* which are calculated to produce upon the observer a stronger sense of their difference than the same observer would receive from lights the sole difference of which lies in their revolutions being performed in greater or less intervals of time. On the other hand, the distinctions derived from time, if the intervals on which they depend do not approach too closely to each other, appear to afford very suitable means for characterizing lights, and the number of distinctions which may be founded upon time alone are pretty numerous. Coloured media have the great disadvantage of absorbing light, and the only colour which has hitherto been found useful in practice is red, all others, at even moderate distances, serving merely to enfeeble, without characterizing, lights. In the system of Fresnel, as already explained, all the distinctions are based upon time alone. Mr Robert Stevenson, the engineer of the Northern Lighthouses, has invented two distinctions, which, although they are produced by variations of the time, possess characteristic *appearances*, sufficiently marked to enable an observer to distinguish a light without counting time. The one is called a *flashing* light, in which the flashes and eclipses succeed each other so rapidly as to give the appearance of a succession of brilliant scintillations, and the other has been called *intermittent*, from its consisting of a fixed light, which is suddenly and totally eclipsed, and again as suddenly revealed to view. The effect of this light is entirely different from that of any revolving light, both from the great inequality of the intervals of light and darkness and also from the contrast which is produced by its sudden disappearance and reappearance, which is completely different from the gradual diminution and increase of the light in revolving lights, more especially in those on the catoptric principle. The great and still increasing number of lights renders the means of distinguishing them one of the most important considerations connected with lighthouses

Arrangement of
lights on
the coast

Not less important, and very nearly allied to the subject of distinction, is that of the arrangement of lights on a line of coast. The choice of the most suitable places, and the assigning to each the characteristic appearances which are most likely to distinguish it from all the neighbouring lights, are points requiring much consideration, and it ought never to be forgotten, that the indiscriminate erection of lighthouses soon leads to confusion, and that the needless exhibition of a light, by involving the loss of a distinction, may afterwards prove inconvenient in the case of some future light, which time and the growing wants of trade may call for on the same line of coast. To enter at length upon this topic, or even to lay down the general principles which ought to regulate the distribution of lights, would exceed the limits of this article; but in connection with this it may be observed, that the superintendence of lighthouses should be committed to one general body, and ought not to be left to local trusts, whose operations are too often conducted on narrow principles, without reference to general interests. The inconveniences arising from interference between the distinctions of the lights under one trust, and those of the lights under another, are thereby avoided, and the full advantage is obtained of the means of distinction at the disposal of both.

The considerations which enter into the choice of the position and character of the lights on a line of coast are either, on the one hand, so simple and self-evident as

scarcely to admit of being stated in a general form, without becoming mere truisms; or are, on the other hand, so very numerous, and often so complicated, as scarcely to be susceptible of compression into any general laws. We shall not, therefore, do more than very briefly notice, in the form of distinct propositions, a few of the chief considerations which should guide us in the selection of the sites and characteristic appearance of the lighthouses to be placed on a line of coast.

1 The most prominent points of a line of coast, or those first made on over-sea voyages, should be first lighted, and the most powerful lights should be adapted to them, so that they may be discovered by the mariner as long as possible before his reaching land. 2. So far as is consistent with a due attention to distinction, revolving lights of some description, which are necessarily more powerful than fixed lights, should be employed at the outposts on a line of coast. 3 Lights of precisely identical character and appearance should not, if possible, occur within a less distance than 100 miles of each other on the same line of coast, which is made by over-sea vessels. 4 In all cases, the distinction of colour should never be adopted except from absolute necessity. 5. Fixed lights, and others of less power, may be more readily adopted in narrow seas, because the *range* of the lights in such situations is generally less than that of open sea-lights. 6 In narrow seas, also, the distance between lights of the same appearance may often be safely reduced within much lower limits than is desirable for the greater sea-lights. Thus there are many instances in which the distance separating lights of the same character need not exceed 50 miles, and peculiar cases occur in which even a much less separation between similar lights may be sufficient. 7 Lights intended to guard vessels from reefs, shoals, or other dangers, should, in every case where it is practicable, be placed *seaward* of the danger itself, as it is desirable that seamen be enabled to *make* the lights with confidence. 8 Views of economy in the first cost of a lighthouse should never be permitted to interfere with placing it in the best possible position, and, when funds are deficient, it will generally be found that the wise course is to delay the work until a sum shall have been obtained sufficient for the erection of the lighthouse on the best site. 9 The elevation of the lantern above the sea should not, if possible, for sea-lights, exceed 200 feet, and about 150 feet is sufficient, under almost any circumstances, to give the range which is required. Lights placed on high headlands are subject to be frequently wrapped in fog, and are often thereby rendered useless at times when lights on a lower level might be perfectly efficient. But this rule must not, and indeed cannot, be strictly followed, especially on the British coast, where there are so many projecting cliffs, which, while they subject the lights placed on them to occasional obscuration by fog, would also entirely and permanently hide from view lights placed on the lower land adjoining them. In such cases, all that can be done is carefully to weigh all the circumstances of the locality, and choose that site for the lighthouse which seems to afford the greatest balance of advantage to navigation. As might be expected, in questions of this kind, the opinions of the most experienced persons are often very conflicting, according to the value which is set on the various elements which enter into the inquiry. 10 The best position for a sea-light ought rarely to be neglected for the sake of the more immediate benefit of some neighbouring port, however important or influential; and the interests of navigation, as well as the true welfare of the port itself, will generally be much better served by placing the sea-light *where it ought to be*, and adding, on a smaller scale, such subsidiary lights as the channel leading to the entrance of the port may require. 11 It may be held as a general maxim, that the fewer lights that can be employed in the illumination of a coast the

Lightfoot better, not only on the score of economy, but also of real efficiency. Every light needlessly erected may, in certain circumstances, become a source of confusion to the mariner, and, in the event of another light being required in the neighbourhood, it becomes a *deduction* from the means of distinguishing it from the lights which existed previous to its establishment. By the needless erection of a new lighthouse, therefore, we not only expend public treasure, but waste the means of distinction among the neighbouring lights. 12. Distinctions of lights, founded upon the minute estimation of intervals of time between flashes, and especially on the measurement of the duration of light and dark periods, are less satisfactory to the great majority of coasting seamen, and are more liable to derangement by atmospheric changes, than those distinctions which are founded on what may more properly be called the *characteristic appearance* of the lights, in which the times for the recurrence of certain appearances differ so widely from each other as not to require for their detection any very minute observation in a stormy night. Thus, for example, flashing lights of five seconds' interval, and revolving lights of half a minute, one minute, and two minutes, are much more characteristic than those which are distinguished from each other by intervals varying according to a slower series of 5″, 10″, 20″, 40″, &c. 13. Harbour and local lights, which have a circumscribed range, should generally be fixed instead of revolving, and may often, for the same reason, be safely distinguished by coloured media. In many cases, also, where they are to serve as guides into a narrow channel, the leading lights which are used should, at the same time, be so arranged as to serve for a distinction from any neighbouring lights. 14. Floating lights, which are very expensive, and more or less uncertain, from their liability to drift from their moorings, as well as defective in power, should never be employed to indicate a turning-point in a navigation in any situation where the conjunction of lights on the shore can be applied at a reasonable expense.

British and Irish Lights

In concluding, it may be necessary to state that the English lights are placed under the Corporation of Trinity House of Deptford, Stroud, the Scottish lights are under the management of the Commissioners of Northern Lights; and the Irish lights are under the care of the Corporation for preserving and improving the port of Dublin, commonly called the Ballast Board.

Last act of parliament, 16th and 17th Vict. cap 131. The last act of parliament on the subject of lighthouses forms part of one of the general title of which is, " An act to amend various laws relating to merchant shipping." It passed 20th August 1853. The chief provisions which affect lighthouses are the following:—1 The light dues of the United

Kingdom are to form one *imperial* fund, under the control of the Board of Trade. 2 From this fund all expenses of erecting and maintaining the lights of the United Lightfoot Kingdom are to be defrayed. 3 The three boards which manage the lighthouses in England, Scotland, and Ireland are to render account of their expenditure to the Board of Trade. 4 The Trinity House, or English board, is to exercise a certain control over the boards in Scotland and Ireland, and is to judge of all their proposals to erect new lights, or to change existing ones, but in every case the sanction of the Board of Trade must precede the acts of each of the three boards.

The following works may be consulted on the subject of lighthouses:—Smeaton's *Narrative of the Eddystone Lighthouse*, Lond 1793, Stevenson's *Account of the Bell-Rock Lighthouse*, Edinburgh, 1824, Belidor, *Architecture Hydraulique*, vol iv, p 151, Peclet, *Traité de l éclairage des Phares*, Paris, 1827, Fresnel s *Mémoire sur un Nouveau Système d éclairage des Phares*, Paris, 1822, Admiral de Rossel s *Rapport*, contenant *l'Exposition du Système adopté par la Commission des Phares pour éclairer les Cotes de France*, Paris, 1825, *Treatise on Burning Instruments* containing the method of building large polyzonal lenses, by D Brewster, LL D, F R S, Edin 1812, *Fanale di Salvore, nell' Istria, Illuminato a Gaz*, Vienna, 1821, *On Construction of Polyzonal Lenses and Mirrors of Great Magnitude, for Lighthouses*, &c, by D Brewster, LL D, F R S (*Edin Phil Jour*, 1823 vol viii, p 160), *Account of a New System of Illumination for Lighthouses*, by D Brewster, LL D, F R S, Edin 1827, *Saggio di Osservazione*, &c, or Observations on the Means of Improving the Construction of Lighthouses, with an Appendix, on the Application of Gas to Lighthouses, by the Chevalier G Aldini, Milan, 1823, Bordier Marcet s *Notice descriptif d un Fanal à double aspect*, &c Paris, 1823, Bordier Marcet s *Parabole Soumise à l art, ou Essai sur la Catoptrique de l éclairage*, Paris, 1819, L Fresnel s *Description Sommaire des Phares et Fanaux allumés sur les Cotes de France, au 1er d Août*, 1837 *The Lighthouses of the British Islands, from the Hydrographical Office of the Admiralty*, Lond 1836, *Instructions pour le service des Phares Lenticulaires*, par L Fresnel, Paris, 1836, Stevenson s *Sketch of Civil Engineering in America*, London, 1838, p 296, *Report of Select Committee of the House of Commons on Lighthouses* 1834, *Report by a Committee of the Board to the Commissioners of the Northern Lighthouses, on the "Report of the Select Committee,'* 1836, *Report to the Commissioners of the Northern Lighthouses on the Illumination of Lighthouses*, by Alan Stevenson, M A, Edin, 1834, *Report to the same Board, on the Inchkeith Dioptric Light*, by Alan Stevenson, Edin, 1835, *Report on the Isle of May Dioptric Light*, by Alan Stevenson, 1836, *Report on the Isle of May Light* by a *Committee of the Royal Society* (Professor Forbes, reporter), Edin 1836, *Account of Skerryvore Lighthouse, with Notes on Lighthouse Illumination*, by Alan Stevenson, LL B, Edin, A & C Black, 1847 Stevenson s *Treatise on the History, Construction and Illumination of Lighthouses*, London, 1850, *Account of the Holophotal System of Illuminating Lighthouses*, by Thomas Stevenson, F R S E, C E, in the *Transactions of the Royal Scottish Society of Arts* for 1849, *Formulæ for Constructing Totally Reflecting Hemispherical Mirrors*, by William Swan F R S E, *Trans Roy Scott Soc of Arts*, 1850, *Description of Spherico-Cylindric Lenses*, &c, by T Stevenson, F R S E, *Edinburgh New Philosophical Journal* 1855, *Report of the Lighthouse Board of America*, Washington, 1852   (A S—N)

LIGHTFOOT, JOHN, a learned commentator, was the son of a clergyman, and was born at the rectory of Stoke-upon-Trent, in March 1602. After receiving his elementary education at Moreton Green, near Congleton, he entered, in 1617, Christ's College, Cambridge, where he applied himself to the study of the learned languages, and was reputed the best orator among the under-graduates. At the age of nineteen he became Bachelor of Arts, and leaving the university, acted as usher for two years in a school at Repton, in Derbyshire. He then took orders, and was appointed curate of Norton-under-Hales, in Shropshire. While chaplain in the family of Sir Rowland Cotton, he became imbued with an enthusiasm for the study of Hebrew; and shortly afterwards resigning his cure, he removed to London in order to devote his time wholly to study. Here, after a short stay, he formed the design of

travelling abroad, but was prevailed on to become pastor of Stone, in his native county. This charge he quitted in 1628, a short time after his marriage, and removed to Hornsey, near London, for the purpose of consulting Sion College Library in the course of his studies. In 1629 appeared his first work, *Erubhim, or Miscellanies, Christian and Judaical*. Sir Rowland Cotton, to whom it was dedicated, presented him, in 1630, to the rectory of Ashley, in Staffordshire.

Lightfoot now devoted himself ardently and exclusively to the study of the Scriptures, and in order to superintend the publication of his researches, he, in 1642, again repaired to London, where he was appointed minister of St Bartholomew, behind the Exchange. On account of his great biblical learning, he was nominated a member of the Assembly of Divines, and in their councils he was a bold and

CPSIA information can be obtained at www.ICGtesting.com

227508LV00004B/68/P